Anne Thorntons
Insider's Guide to Home Improvement

Professional Tips to Maintain Your Home

Marriah Publishing
122 Manners Road
Ringoes, NJ 08551

ISBN - 978-1-945853-17-3

THANK YOU

Thank you, thank you, thank you to an amazing team of family, colleagues and friends who inspire me every day!

Also, thank you to the audiences who have attended my in-person Home Maintenance Tip presentations. You are the reason for this updated version of my book. Your questions, insights, stories and suggestions given at every one of my presentations has helped to add a great deal of new information in the 2019 issue of my Insider's Guide to Home Improvement (property insurance, babyproofing your home, garage organization, vacation checklist, remodeling for older people to stay in their homes longer, landscape and landscape irrigation, smart homes, plus updated home maintenance tips).

Of course, I must thank Colleen Kelly and Jeanne Murphy of Marriah Media, publishers of my book. Together they are a mighty team! Colleen, you have once again literally brought this book to life with layout and design. And Jeanne, your support and encouragement continues to be unwavering and so appreciated. Thank you ladies! Let's not forget Sally Montana for the beautiful photographs! @SallyMontana

Finally, to all of my co-workers at MSI Plumbing & Remodeling. You are all a testament to the hard work we do every day for our customers. A big giant THANK YOU for all you do!

4

TABLE OF CONTENTS

TABLE OF CONTENTS

TABLE OF CONTENTS

TABLE OF CONTENTS

TABLE OF CONTENTS

TABLE OF CONTENTS

PREFACE

THE KNOWLEDGEABLE HOMEOWNER

Home repair and remodeling is a daunting task for any homeowner – no matter who you are. Most people hate it! And women in particular feel overwhelmed at the prospect of even the most basic home repair. Why? Because many women just don't have the basic information about their home's building systems. They feel vulnerable and know that they could be taken advantage of by the wrong contractor. That is why I have written this book.

This is what I have learned over my 30 years in the plumbing and remodeling business: being knowledgeable, prepared and proactive can make a HUGE difference in both the severity of a problem and the cost to repair that problem.

My Insider's Guide to Home Improvement will help you learn how to choose a contractor, identify and correct possible problems, create a maintenance calendar, and help you build a vocabulary of "building terms" so you will feel more confident when you do interact with contractors.

I've learned a lot over the years from my team of professional plumbers, electricians, designers, remodelers, carpenters, painters, tile artisans and other related contractors. They have taught me that there really is a lot that you can do as a homeowner to monitor and maintain your home. When you follow these tips, reminders, checklists and calendars contained in this book you will definitely stay on top of all of your home repair and remodeling projects, whether you use a contractor or do it yourself.

1 TYPES OF HOME SERVICE COMPANIES

Home repair service companies includes plumbers, electricians, carpenters, masons, heating and air conditioning technicians, landscapers and landscape irrigation technicians, appliance technicians, siding/window companies, driveway/paving companies and pool companies, among others. Service companies are just that. You call them when you need a particular service -- your faucet is leaking, your furnace stopped working, your patio is falling apart. Probably about half the time a service is needed it is an "emergency." The other half of the time it is a "planned" repair.

Home Repair Companies

Home repair service companies might also offer you different types of "service plans" that will keep your equipment running efficiently. Typical service plans include: annual furnace and air conditioning tune ups, periodic plumbing inspections, opening and closing landscape irrigation systems, annual generator service, and annual pool and landscape services, among others.

Home Remodeling Companies

Home remodeling companies can be a variety of sizes and offer a variety of services. Typically, they are "general contractors" who have a few carpenters as "employees" and then they bring together sub "trade" contractors (plumbing, electric, tile, paint, flooring, etc.) to complete a project.

Whether you are working with a repair company or a remodeling company, they should be professional and experienced in the latest building products and technology, assuring you the highest quality job. Lastly, they should be licensed and insured.

Home Inspection Companies

When you are purchasing a new home, you will want to hire a home inspection company to inspect and review all of the home's components. They should provide you with a written report, typically with details and photos of what they find. There are also certifications and licenses for home inspectors. Check with your state to review those requirements, and then make sure the company you hire has all met all of the certifications.

The home inspection report should help point out any necessary repairs or unforeseen costs before you buy. It should also reduce the risks of unwanted "surprises" in your new home.

Typically, the report will cover the following:

- Driveways, soil, sidewalks
- Garage door
- Gutters and downspouts
- Roofs
- Windows and shutters
- Skylights
- Dormers
- Siding
- Chimney and roof vents

- Decks and porches
- Floors and doors
- HVAC, including ductwork
- Foundation
- Basement
- Sump pump and pit
- Stairs and handrails
- Plumbing
- Electric

DISASTER RESPONSE COMPANIES

You want to be ready BEFORE a disaster strikes your home. Disaster response companies respond 24 hours a day, 365 days a year to literally any kind of disaster. These companies will respond to fires, floods, pipe breaks, sewage spills, and all kinds of storms. Many will even respond to biohazards, trauma scenes, chemical and hazmat spills and animal infestation clean up and decontamination.

If you have a disaster, you want the most knowledgeable and skilled technicians responding with state of the art tools and equipment. Clean up, restoration, remediation and reconstruction is a huge process with many components. Make sure the company is licensed and certified in your state. Many companies also use products that can address a customer's environmental allergies and sensitivities.

DISASTER ZONE

It was April 29. Erin and Sean were celebrating their wedding anniversary. Erin thought it would be romantic to draw a bath, but while the water was running Sean surprised her with flowers and dinner from their favorite restaurant (and a Sam Smith song playing on his phone). As they ate dinner, suddenly a drop of water hit the table between them. When they looked up, it was coming from the ceiling. It was at that moment Erin realized that she never turned the water off on the tub and it had overflowed, flooding their master bath! Sean and Erin needed a disaster response company and they had no idea who to call. Now, let's learn how to not be like Sean and Erin!

How To Choose The Right Companies For You

There are many ways to identify the best contractor for the job, and it is easier than you think to be prepared for the worst. See the Appendix for a Contractor Evaluation Form. Here are my most important tips.

The worst time to look for a home repair company is in an emergency. If you don't already have a list of companies to call, ask your neighbors, colleagues, do some research online, but find several reputable companies to call BEFORE your emergency. When someone has an emergency, they just usually go to the internet or phone book and start calling multiple companies to see who responds first. A company may respond first, but they might not have proper licenses, trained personnel or the right insurance, etc. And, this stuff matters! All kinds of things can go wrong in a home repair or remodel situation. So, when you hire a sub-par company, you are exposing yourself not only to shoddy work but to situations that might require insurance. If the contractor doesn't have the right insurance, the homeowner will be responsible if there is some type of claim.

Tip #1

Research your contractor.

There are many ways to research a contractor. The internet (Angie's List, Yelp, other review sites) Better Business Bureau, Chamber of Commerce and other local business organizations. Also, visit your local township Building Code office and ask for recommendations. If the trade is licensed like plumbing, electrical, etc., contact your state office of licensing for information about the contractor. And, always get at least 3 forms of contact information – email, cell phone, mailing address, website address, fax, office phone.

Tip #2

Verify their professional licenses & certifications.

For licensed trades like plumbing, electrical, home inspector, pest control, heating/air conditioning, etc., always ask for a copy of their license. Many licensed trades also have industry certifications; you should ask for copies of those and make verifications. Often their knowledge and experience can save you time, money and aggravation. For example, if you are purchasing a whole-house generator (which can cost from $5,000 to $20,000), you will want that contractor to have been trained and certified in the installation of that particular manufacturer's product and be trained in providing ongoing maintenance of the equipment needed to ensure your investment is protected.

Tip #3

ALWAYS have a contract.

In New Jersey, any job over $1,000 not only requires a written contract by law, but the contract language itself is required to cover certain areas regarding job and material specifications, payments, warranties, insurance, etc. You would think that a "word of mouth" recommendation is the best thing. But in reality most bad contractor experiences stem from the recommendation of a neighbor or family/friend. Because when someone you know recommends a company or person it provides a level of comfort and causes you to skip formalities like a signed contract, proper licensing, defined scope of work and a project timeline. So, when something goes wrong, you feel uncomfortable confronting the situation AND you have no legal ground to stand on. Regardless of how many friends, family members, or co-workers swear by a contractor's work, verbal agreements do not supersede a written contract. Horror stories about "word of mouth" type deals are more frequent than you can imagine. And, they all end badly for the homeowner because they either got scammed or the job was substandard. This is an important distinction. According to the Better Business Bureau scammers take off with your money without ever completing the job and substandard work is just that: substandard. Either way, if you don't have a signed contract, you have no possible relief at all. See appendix for sample Scope of Work. Consult with your state about what should be included in a residential home improvement contract.

Tip #4

For major projects get at least 3 in-home estimates.

After you have done your research, ask at least 3 contractors to give you an estimate for the work. Three estimates will help you find the fair market value of your project. Make sure that all estimates are broken down into "labor" costs and "material" costs so that you can really compare apples to apples. And, remember…while a low estimate may look like a good deal, it's probably a headache waiting to happen. Dismiss estimates that are oddly low because the contractor is either cutting corners or doesn't have proper insurance or licensing or both. The old adage certainly applies to the remodeling industry – You Get What You Pay For!

Tip #5

NEVER pay in full up front.

No reputable contractor or repairperson will ask you to pay everything in full before the job even starts! Most large remodeling jobs are paid over time as the work is done and the appropriate inspections are passed. A typical contract will request 25% at signing of contract, 25% to start the job, 25% when rough inspections are passed, 23% when complete and 2% after final inspections are received. Other contractors like the 1/3, 1/3, 1/3 method of payment. It's really a negotiating point for you to determine your own method of payment. Also, in larger remodeling jobs where sub contractors are involved, it is important to have a Lien Waiver in place, signed by the General Contractor and all the sub-contractors. In New Jersey, if you don't have a Lien Waiver in place and your General Contractor doesn't pay the sub contractor, the sub contractor can file a Lien against YOUR property! Which means you can not sell your property until the Lien has been satisfied. The Lien Waiver is filled out by the General Contractor and sub contractor(s), who confirm that they have been paid for the work on your behalf. This form is important and it will protect you. A copy of a typical Lien Waiver can be found in the Appendix.

Here are some other things to think about as you are evaluating a company.

- Did they show up on time?
- Were they wearing company apparel?
- Does their truck have the business name, phone number and license numbers required?
- Did they offer a business card and/or other company marketing material?
- Did they bring a camera or tablet to take photos?
- Did they take measurements?
- Did they tell you a range of costs for your project?
- Did they tell you when they would have their estimate ready?

? Here are 17 questions to ask the prospective contractor. ?

1) Who owns the business & how long have you been in business?	2) Are you involved in the local Chamber of Commerce, other local business groups or a national trade association?	3) Are you licensed in your state, as required? What licenses? Get copies of licenses.	4) How many projects like mine have you completed in the last year?
5) May I have a list of references from those projects?	6) Can I visit a prior customer's job to see a finished product?	7) May I have a list of business referrals and suppliers?	8) What percentage of your business is repeat or referral business?
9) Does your company carry worker's compensation and liability insurance? Do all of your sub contractors have the appropriate insurance? Get copies of certificates of insurance from the general contractor and the sub contractors.	10) Will building permits be required for my project? Most projects require inspections for building, plumbing, fire, electric, and some projects need to be submitted to your local Zoning and Health Department for approval as well. Before you even ask the contractor this question, you can visit your local Building Department and ask them. Then you can verify what the contractor tells you.	11) Who will be assigned as project supervisor for the job?	12) Who will be working on the project? Get names of employees and subcontractors.
13) What is your approach to a project such as this?	14) How long will it take for my project from start to finish?	15) What kind of "unexpected" expenses are expected?	16) How do you handle the "dirty work" of dust containment?

17) Will you be providing a written contract with the following?

a) details of the job (including product specifications) b) a breakdown of costs by labor and materials
c) list of sub contractors and their insurance   d) how change orders are handled
e) payment schedule & 3-day right to cancel clause   f) written warranties
g) project start and end date

18

2 SINGLE FAMILY HOMES, CONDOS, BUILDING CODES AND INSURANCE

Basic Building Components

Whether you own a single family home or condominium or rent an apartment, the building's systems are the same, i.e., roofing, siding, electric, plumbing, etc. The question is who is responsible to pay for maintenance, repairs and replacement of any of these systems or their components?

If you live in a residence that you own, the answer is simple – YOU!

If you live (own or rent) in a condominium or other multi-family living arrangement, the answer is more complicated and will depend on your association's legal documents and adopted guidelines, which outline those responsibilities. For the most part, the interior maintenance, repairs and replacements are the responsibility of the homeowner. Typically, your association takes care of almost all of the exterior issues. However, checking your association's particular documents will detail who is really responsible.

Municipal Building Codes

Municipal building codes and requirements can sometimes be more stringent if you live in a condominium association or apartment complex because of the safety involved in multi-unit housing. For example, local municipalities may have different permit requirements for multi-unit housing communities. Always check with your town, township or county for your particular area.

⚠️ DISASTER ZONE ⚠️

Bob and Lisa needed a new furnace. They got a post card in the mail for what looked like a good contractor. When they talked to the salesman, they asked whether a permit was necessary in their town. The salesman told them that he wasn't sure and if they wanted a permit, they could inquire but so many people don't like having strangers in their homes and don't bother. They decided to check with the building official and learned that the permit was required and by getting one, it assures that the installers will not cut corners because they know their work will be inspected by a third party to verify everything was done correctly. Be like Bob and Lisa, always check to avoid disaster.

Renting an Apartment, Single Family House or Condominium
Tips for Tenants

It is important to know your rights as a tenant, whether you rent an apartment, single family house or a condominium. Rules and requirements can vary with each style of property. For example, condominium associations can have a whole list of requirements for their residents. Here's a list of suggestions and questions to ask to make the process more organized and successful.

Paperwork is King!

Being prepared will definitely win over a landlord. Bring your completed rental application, references from other landlords and maybe even from your employer. Some landlords will also want your credit report so make sure and have the latest one available. You can order your credit report online at www.annualcreditreport.com or you can get your reports directly from the websites of the three major national credit bureaus:

Equifax: www.equifax.com

Experian: www.experian.com

TransUnion: www.transunion.com

Ask questions upfront.

You want to make sure you have a full picture of the property, the rules and the neighborhood. Here are some questions you will definitely want to ask:

- What is the monthly rent?
- What is included in the rent? (Any utilities, garbage, recycling, recreational amenities, parking spots, etc?)
- What is the square footage of the residence?
- What is the level of "sound" inside the residence?
- What is the neighborhood like? Plan to visit during the day, evening and the weekend as neighborhoods can change.
- What is the security deposit amount and how long does it take to get it back once you move out?
- Can I paint the walls?
- Can I put up holiday lights on the balcony or around the front door?
- Ask what the process is to get any improvements done (upgrading appliances or new carpet, etc.).

Review the lease (all of it).

I can't stress enough how important it is to review the entire lease. And, if you feel uncomfortable or don't understand something, have a friend, colleague or lawyer review it too. You want to make sure that there aren't any clauses that might restrict you. For example, restrictions on guests or pets or running a home business. Get EVERYTHING in writing. If a verbal conversation takes place about the landlord making a repair, immediately afterwards send the landlord a written confirmation of your conversation. Keep copies of everything.

In order to protect your security deposit, consider taking photos of every room as you do the initial walk through with the landlord (before you move in). Keep those photos for reference when you move out!

Know and protect your privacy rights.

Check with your state to make sure you know the rights you have to privacy in a space that you rent. You want to know when a landlord has the right to enter your rental unit and if they need to give you advance notice.

Ask for repairs in writing.

Landlords have certain legal requirements to provide a habitable rental unit to their renters. Basic requirements include heat, water, electricity, and a clean and structurally safe environment. If you need repairs, always put your request in writing. Include photos and descriptions of problems too.

Always purchase renter's insurance.

If you have a loss (of your personal items) due to theft or damage, your landlord's property insurance will not cover the loss. Renter's insurance is relatively cheap and can protect you in the event of theft, damage caused by other people and natural disasters.

Insurance for Your Home or Rental

Whether you rent an apartment or purchase a home or condo, an insurance policy will protect your investment from risks such as fire, lightning, or theft. The type of insurance policy you obtain depends on the type of property you're insuring. Homeowners can choose between a Special Form (HO-3) and Comprehensive Form (HO-5); renters can obtain a Contents Broad Form (HO-4); and condo owners can obtain a Condominium Unit-Owners Form (HO-6).

Mortgage companies typically require you to purchase an insurance policy and pay the first year's premium in full prior to closing. The premium is based on a number of factors, including policy coverages and endorsements.

Every policy has a deductible. That means that if you experience a covered loss and need to file a claim, you must pay a specified amount of money before an insurance company will pay.

Coverage A: Dwelling

For homeowners, this provides coverage for the dwelling and any structures attached to it, while used as a private residence. To completely protect a home, the coverage limit should equal the cost to fully rebuild the home, which might differ from its selling price. A replacement cost analysis accounts for the home's square footage, number of stories, type of construction, age, and other relevant characteristics.

For condo owners, this protects interior walls and attached upgrades (such as cabinets and carpets). A condo association master policy will cover the outside of the structure. As a condo owner, it is your responsibility to understand: 1) what the association policy covers; 2) what the association policy deductible is, and how it impacts you if you experience a loss; and 3) what your HO-6 policy covers.

Coverage B: Other Structures

For homeowners policies only, this covers structures on your property that are not attached to your home (such as a detached garage or storage shed).

Coverage C: Personal Property

Coverage for items you own or use (such as furniture, clothing, and kitchenware).

Coverage D: Loss of Use

Coverage for additional expenses you'd incur if your home became uninhabitable as a result of a covered loss.

Homeowners, condo owners, and renters policies also include coverage for liability:

Coverage E: Personal Liability

Coverage for bodily injury or property damage for which you are found liable.

Coverage F: Medical Payments to Others

Coverage for medical expenses you'd incur by others (such as someone tripping on your porch and breaking their wrist).

Coverages E and F do not apply to resident family members of your household.

In addition, you can customize your policy to obtain higher coverage limits through endorsements such as:

- *Scheduled Personal Property* – Sometimes referred to as a rider or jewelry insurance, this provides greater protection from theft for certain high-value items such as jewelry and watches.

- *Credit Card, Fund Transfer Card, Forgery, and Counterfeit Money Coverage* – Increases the limit of homeowners insurance coverage if you experience a loss due to a forged check, counterfeit money, or fraudulent use of your credit card.

Workers' Compensation Insurance

It is your responsibility as a homeowner to confirm that all contractors who work for you have workers' compensation insurance coverage. Ask your contractors for a Certificate of Insurance, which is readily available from their insurance agent. And, if your contractor is using a sub-contractor, ask for a copy of the sub-contractor's Certificate of Insurance as well.

Special thanks to NJM Insurance Group for providing this information.

Most of the items in this book deal with tips that will help you take care of the physical aspects of your home to maintain and grow its value. The following tips are far more important because they will help keep you and your family safe and healthy.

Check Your Smoke Detectors And Carbon Monoxide Alarms On A Regular Basis

Newer ones have expiration dates printed right on them. Make sure you have enough and that they are working. You want to test them periodically and make sure that they can be heard in all parts of your house. Push and hold the test button for a few seconds. The detector should produce a loud noise. To test whether the unit will actually work in a fire, you can purchase a small spray can of "smoke detector test aerosol" at most hardware stores. Follow the directions. If your alarm does not go off, even if it beeps when you hold the button down, it is a non-functioning smoke detector. Try changing the batteries and cleaning the detector to remove any dust, then repeat the procedure. If it doesn't work again, replace the unit as soon as possible. And, remember, even hard-wired smoke detectors have backup batteries that must be replaced! A common reminder is to change the batteries for daylight savings time in the spring and fall.

Clogged Dryer Vents Cause Fires!

More than 15,000 dryer vent fires occur every year in the United States. Dryer vent fires are a real problem in newer, bigger homes where the dryer is placed in the center of the house and not up against an outside wall. Some of these dryer vents can run 15, 20, 25 feet to exhaust to the outside — that's a lot of length with twists and turns. Here are some of the signs that it's time to not only clean your vent, but to check out the pipe run in the attic looking for kinks, holes, etc.

- Clothes are not completely dry.
- You smell a musty odor in the clothing.
- Clothing seems unusually hot to the touch after a complete drying cycle.
- The dryer vent hood flap does not properly open as it is designed to do during the operation of the dryer.
- Debris is noticed within the outside dryer vent opening.
- It gets very hot in the laundry room.
- There is a lot of lint in the trap.

DISASTER ZONE

When Michael and Jeff remodeled their home with an open concept design, they wanted the laundry to be easily accessible next to the kitchen. What they didn't realize was that by placing the laundry in the middle of the home and not on an outside wall, the dryer vent ran almost 15 feet. They didn't realize the fire hazard and never thought to hire someone to clean the vent. Over time, a clog formed and caused a small fire that could have been easily avoidable.

Chimney Safety

Avoid a chimney fire or puff back (smoke and soot coming into the house) by having your chimney and flue inspected regularly. Reasons for chimney fires or puff backs include leaky, broken or poorly constructed chimneys, crooked pipe layout, blocked passage, air pressure, over-dry firewood and seasonal changes.

Radon Is Alive and Well

Radon is a radioactive gas that is generated through the breakdown of uranium inside the earth. It is invisible, odorless and tasteless, with no immediate health symptoms. According to the American Lung Association radon is the second leading cause of lung cancer in the US, causing about 21,000 lung cancer related deaths annually. When radon is found indoors the odorless gas can accumulate to dangerous levels. Radon can enter your home through cracks in solid floors, construction joints, cracks in walls, gaps in suspended floors, gaps around service pipes, cavities inside walls and your water supply. Get a test kit and test regularly.

Don't Get Burned!

At 140 degrees, it takes 5 seconds for water to burn skin. At 160 degrees, it takes only 1/2 of a second. Home hot water systems should be set to no hotter than 120 degrees.

DISASTER ZONE

Barbara had recently moved into a house built in the 1920s and loved the look of the original wood stove in the living room. She decided to have it inspected and discovered that creosote, the highly combustible residue that sticks to the inner walls, had built up so much that the inspector was shocked that it had not yet caused a house fire. Loving the look of something is one thing – it is quite another to make sure stoves and fireplaces are completely safe (every year).

Do You Have A Fire Extinguisher?

If you don't have a few fire extinguishers in your house, go get some! They come in different sizes too. Keep one in the kitchen area and the garage area. Fire marshals advise to have the fire extinguisher near the exit (NOT IN A CLOSET). Check them annually to make sure they are in good working condition. It's a simple safety investment for you and your family.

Plumbing Torches Start Fires!

Did you know that there is a technology for plumbers to use that DOES NOT INCLUDE a torch of any kind to connect plumbing pipes? This technology has been available to plumbers for over ten years. It is called the "press fit system" and involves a special tool that crimps pipes/fittings together with the force of 3,000 psi. So, the next time you need plumbing work, remember to ask your plumber what they use to connect pipes -- the acetylene torch method or the press fit system. Keep your home and family safe -- make sure your contractors are using the safest tools and materials available to them.

Is it a good idea to shut off water to my whole house when going away?

Absolutely! You will have less of a chance of a water catastrophe if a leak should develop. This way, only what is in the pipes will leak out.

Key Safety

Have you recently moved into a new home? Make sure you immediately change the locks and make spare keys. There's no way of knowing how many copies of your old key may be floating around. And, don't HIDE your keys on your property. Most burglars know where to look.

Garage Door Openers

If you have a garage door opener, it is important to make sure the auto-reverse feature is in working order. This feature can keep your garage door from being damaged – or damaging any of your personal property, family members or pets.

Preventing Falls

One of the most important things you can do in your home is to try and prevent falls. This is a great list to get your started.

- Improve visibility at night with low wattage night lights near bedrooms, bathrooms and stairs.
- Add motion detector lighting to your exterior.
- Install nonslip mats or tack strips in bathtubs.
- Install grab bars and handrails in bathrooms.
- Apply sand-finish polyurethane for traction on wooden stairs.
- On exterior sidewalks, brush finish the concrete for improved traction.
- Purchase a space saving, folding step ladder. It will be so much safer than standing on a chair!

Emergency Preparedness

Here is a list of emergency supplies to always have on hand.

- Flashlights & extra batteries
- Battery-operated radio
- First aid kit
- Extra non-perishable food and water
- Essential medicines
- Cell phone with portable charger

VACATION CHECKLIST

Check these off your list and have a great vacation!

- Make your house look like someone is home.
- Have a trusted neighbor take care of newspapers, mail, etc. or ask the post office to put your mail on hold. Make sure your neighbor knows your vacation plans for any emergency contact. Ask them to park their car in your driveway.
- Get all your trash and recycling together and ask your neighbor to put it out on trash day and then put the empty containers back in your garage or storage area on the same day. (You're going to owe your neighbor a nice thank you gift!)
- Arrange to have your lawn mowed (or snow shoveled) while you're away.
- Turn the water off to your house!
- Never leave bikes or scooters lying around your home or property.
- Never leave your house key hidden outside your home.
- Make sure all the doors, windows and skylights are closed and locked.
- Set timers on interior lights. Install exterior motion-detection lighting.
- Close blinds and curtains tightly.
- Set the heating system to provide minimum heat of 55 degrees.
- Make sure to unplug televisions, computers and appliances that are susceptible to lightening and power surges.
- Advise your alarm company and local police if you will be gone for an extended vacation.
- Store jewelry and valuable papers in a safety deposit box.
- Any valuable that can be hocked (like electronic equipment and computers) should not be visible from windows. If a thief can't see something that can be easily converted to cash, they will probably move on to the next house.
- Never announce your vacation plans on social networks.

BABYPROOFING **YOUR HOME**

As you plan to babyproof your home, remember to consider all the stages of a child's development: pulling up on furniture, crawling, walking, running and climbing.

Before you begin to research products that are specific to helping you babyproof your home, start with these home safety basics that will keep everyone in your family safe.

- Make sure you have up to date fire extinguishers and that you know how to use them!
- Your water heater temperature should be at or below 120 degrees.
- Are your smoke and carbon monoxide detectors up to date and tested regularly?
- Look around your home, inside and out, for tripping hazards. Then, remove or repair them. Anti-slip mats will help tremendously.
- Check your deck and surrounding area for safety (splinters, broken railings, deck gates, heaved pavers, and other tripping hazards). Keep deck furniture away from railings. Children should never be on a deck alone (especially if your deck is high up).
- Check that your garage door auto-reverse is working correctly.
- Review everything in your garage for safety (remove paint and other hazardous materials to a secure area, make sure garden tools are safely secured).

Basic Baby Proofing for Your Home

- Check all cupboards and drawers for dangerous products (batteries, lighters, matches, detergents, cleaners, vitamin supplements, plant food, dog food and dog products, medicines, etc.). Move these products to upper cabinets for storage. Make sure alcohol is in a locked liquor cabinet.
- Install safety gates where needed.
- Check all drawers for sharp objects and move them to a higher shelf.
- If you keep magnets on your refrigerator, remember to move them up.
- Cover and latch everything in the kitchen and bathrooms! Cabinets, drawers, hinges, stove knobs, basement doors. Make sure cords don't dangle from countertops. Install a toilet lock. Use doorknob covers and locks.
- Check all latches on windows and doors. Keep windows locked. Research appropriate window/door baby products. Older homes have special requirements because of larger, more fragile windows and doors. Newer homes have much safer windows. All windows, however, need to be babyproofed.
- Cover all electrical outlets with appropriate covers. DO NOT use plastic electrical "plugs" – they are a known choking hazard. Keep lighting cords tucked and taped out of reach. Use UL listed night lights throughout your home.
- Cover all radiators, heating vents and fireplace hearths. Basically, cover anything with a sharp edge! Including the tub spout.

* Make sure furniture is attached to the wall (book shelves, cabinets, dressers) and that the TV is secured. The "L" bracket is your friend! Move furniture away from windows. Cover any sharp edges on coffee tables, end tables, chairs, etc.
* Check all doorstops. Some have removable caps that can be a choking hazard.
* Install cordless blinds (cords are strangling hazards).
* Houseplants should be out of reach.
* Just put away all the knick knacks. You'll be glad you did!

Remodeling To Age In Place

There are many things you can do to help someone age in place. The main thing is to make the home environment as safe as possible. And, remember, as someone ages, they will also have different needs for their home. Here are some of the most important things to think about.

- Fire extinguishers (make sure senior knows how to use one).
- Install new fire & carbon monoxide detectors with a ten year battery life.
- Bathtubs and showers can be dangerous. Consider installing a walk in tub.
- Install handheld shower heads with adjustable settings.
- Toilets should be chair height for ease of use.
- Non slip flooring should be considered for all areas of the home.
- If you are doing a complete remodel, consider the height adjustments for sinks, toilets, and counters. Always consider for a wheelchair, so include knee clearance to get to and from the sink and wider doorways.

- Remodel a closet for easier access to hanging clothes and drawers.
- For help with mobility install grab bars and handrails wherever the homeowner might need them (near toilet, bathtub, showers, chairs, bed, etc.).
- Install light fixtures that are easy to turn on and off.
- For stairs and other elevation changes in the home, install non-skid reflective tape.
- Light switches can be lowered for easier access. Also, electrical outlets can be raised for easier access.
- Installing ramps wherever needed.
- Have your plumber install anti-scalding devices on faucets.
- Replace door knobs with door lever handles.

Consider rounded countertop edges which provide safer walkways.

Install low pile carpet or laminate floors making it easier to walk or get around in a wheelchair.

Seniors need more light. Remove heavy window coverings and allow natural light in.

Install window blinds to alter the direction and amount of natural light entering the home.

Light up all the exterior areas with motion detectors and lights on timers.

Tuck away flashlights in every room for easy access.

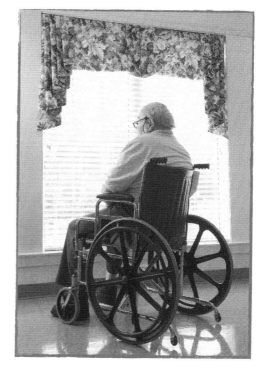

Put nightlights in every room.

Encourage the seniors in your life to be aware of their surroundings for their safety.

Plumbing Components

There are three basic parts to the home's plumbing system.

- Water supply pipes: distribute water throughout the house (hot and cold).
- Fixtures that use water: faucets, toilets, appliances.
- Wastewater management: Drain-waste-vent system that carries wastewater out of the house.

How to turn the water off in an emergency.

Do your research before an emergency. Know that there are two different kinds of valves.

Globe or Gate Valve with
Wagon Wheel Style Handle

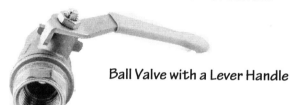

Ball Valve with a Lever Handle

It is highly recommended that all your valves be ball, lever handle style valves. They are more dependable and almost never fail. Keep this in mind as you locate your own water valves in your home.

Turn Off Directions For City Water

1. Locate water meter (typically in your basement or lowest level of your house and typically on the front wall).
2. There will be a valve before and after it.
3. First, turn the valve that is downsteam (house side) of the meter (the meter will have a directional arrow on it). If this valve works, then no need to check the upstream side (street or curb shut off valve). However, it is important to know where the "curb" shut off valve is located outside. Ask your water company if you can't find it.
4. Again, if the inside shut off valve is a wagon wheel valve, consider changing it to a ball valve with a lever style handle.

Turn Off Directions For Well Water

1. Locate your well tank.
2. Find the copper or plastic vertical water line leaving the tank (there will be a shut off valve on this pipe). It will look like a wagon wheel or a lever handle valve.
3. For globe or gate valve with a wheel style handle, turn it clockwise until it can't move anymore. With the wheel style handle, they can fail easily. If at all possible, change it to a lever handle (which almost never fails). If you can not turn the wheel handle at all, then definitely get it changed.
4. For a lever style handle turn it 90 degrees until the handle is perpendicular to the pipe. (Typically, it will only turn in one direction).

Types of Main Water and Water Lines

Copper

In homes across America, copper is the most commonly used main water supply line found today. Copper is actually an essential element for humans (in small amounts). However, too much copper can cause problems, including vomiting, diarrhea, stomach cramps and nausea. Over exposure has also been linked to liver damage and kidney disease. The EPA has established an "action level" for copper in drinking water. The action level for copper is 1.3 mg/L. You can ask your water supplier for the results of their tests for copper.

Lead

Homes built before 1986 are more likely to have lead pipes, fixtures and lead solder. Lead enters your drinking water when service pipes corrode. There is actually NO safe level for lead consumption according to the EPA. The EPA has also established an "action level" for lead in drinking water. The action level for lead is 0.015 mg/L. Here are a few things you can do to reduce your risk of lead poisoning.

- Flush your pipes before drinking (30 seconds to 2 minutes). The longer water "sits" in your pipes, the more lead it can absorb. By flushing the water before using it, you will reduce that risk.
- Use only cold water for eating and drinking (and especially for making baby formula). Hot water is more likely to contain higher levels of lead.
- Boiling water DOES NOT get rid of lead contamination.
- Use water filters or treatment devices. There are many products on the market to treat for lead. Just make sure their claims are verified by independent certifying organizations.

Black Poly (PolyButylene)

PolyButylene is a form of plastic resin that was used from 1978 to 1995. It was originally seen as the "pipe of the future" and was installed in 5 to 10 million homes, especially in the southwestern part of the United States. It was also installed in the Mid-Atlantic and Northwest Pacific area of the U.S. PolyButylene was eventually found to have many weaknesses and in 1995 became UNACCEPTABLE by buildings codes in both the U.S. and Canada.

Pex (Polyethylene)

Pex has been in use in Europe since the 1970s and was introduced in the United States in the 1980s. It has distinct advantages over metal pipe or rigid pipe (PVC) because it is flexible, resistant to scale and chlorine, doesn't corrode or develop pinholes and is faster to install than metal or rigid pipe systems. It also requires fewer connections and fittings.

Understanding Your Well System

There are no valves between the well tank and the incoming line from the well. The underground pump is controlled by a switch down stream of the tank. A valve, accidentally shut off prior to the tank, could cause the incoming pipe to rupture. A check valve is installed on the incoming well line prior to the tank. This device prevents the water and pressure in the tank from draining back into the well when the pump is at rest.

For Gas

1. NEVER try and turn a gas line off (typically you would need a special tool to do this).
2. ALWAYS call a licensed plumber or your local gas utility!

Faucets & Drains

Leaky faucets.

Gone are the days of 10 cent washers. Most modern faucets will require the replacement of an entire cartridge (or 2) to stop a drip. These cartridges are obviously more costly, but last much longer. Some may require specialized tools to remove them from the faucet body. Did you know that the main cause of leaky faucets is worn out washers? The washers inside of the faucet handles are rubber and tend to wear out quickly. Replace them by turning off the main water supply, unscrewing the leaky handle that controls the flow of water to the spout, removing the old washer, and dropping in the new one.

Bathroom sink clogs.

Get a hair strainer for the bathtub drain. If fats and oils are the main source of clogs in the kitchen, hair is the primary culprit in the bathroom. If you have a strainer, make sure that you remove any accumulated hair from it following each shower. This will reduce the amount of hair that finds its way through the strainer and into your plumbing.

Skip the drain cleaners!

Though the acids it contains can help unclog a drain, they also cause significant damage to your plumbing, including premature leaking. This can lead to costly repairs later on. If your bathtub or toilet is completely clogged, use a small drain snake – which you can purchase at any hardware outlet – to pull the offending clog to the surface. If your kitchen sink is clogged, try plunging it before trying to snake the drain. If you cannot remove the clog using a drain snake, call a professional. All household drains can benefit from regular preventative maintenance. A product called Bio-Clean™ is an organic bacteria that should be used on a regular schedule to keep your drains clear.

Cleaning your kitchen sink.

Believe it or not, your kitchen sink can have more bacteria in it than your toilet seat! To disinfect it, clean your sink with soap and water first. Spray a mist of vinegar over it and then spray a mist of hydrogen peroxide. Let it air dry. If your sink is stainless steel, use mineral oil on a cloth to buff out the surface. This helps prevent water stain building up which in turns deters mold.

Double sink, double trouble.

Does your double sink vibrate and make a gong noise? Spray expanding foam between the two sections underneath your sink, let the foam harden and trim away any excess with a knife.

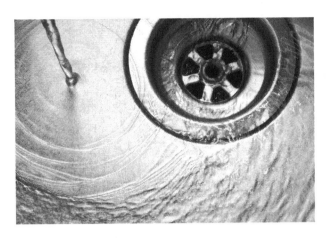

Cleaning your garbage disposal.

The easiest way to clean your garbage disposal is to run it with baking soda and citrus rinds or crushed ice.

Kitchen sink sprayer operation.

If you have to jiggle the hose as your pull out your kitchen sink sprayer, chances are the hose is catching on the shutoff valves. Slip ½ inch foam pipe insulation over the pipes and shut off handles for smooth operation!

Gas Piping

Simply put, gas piping should be left to the professionals. Under NO circumstances do I recommend that a homeowner perform any type of gas piping modification. Far too many hazards exist, as well as the need for specialized equipment and training. And if you ever smell gas, leave and call 911 first and call the utility company second!

Toilets

Toilets account for 27% of your indoor water use. Making sure your toilets are saving water and money is important.

Plunging secrets.

Chances are you've noticed that there are two styles of toilet plungers: standard and flange. The standard plunger has a simple cup, like a half-sphere. The flange plunger has an extension that makes it the more effective choice for plunging toilets.

Low flush toilets save money!

You can save water and money every time you flush your toilet by installing a low-flush toilet. The EPA estimates that the average US home will save up to 18,000 gallons of water per year. That's $90 per year and over $2,000 over the lifetime of the toilet! It's because low flush toilets use less than 1.6 gallons per flush. Remember to only purchase toilets with the EPA's "WaterSense" label which certifies the low flush. Be advised however, that the plumbing in older homes could pose a problem because the plumbing was designed to carry 3 gallons of water instead of 1.6 gallons.

Detect toilet leak with food coloring.

To find out whether your toilet tank is leaking, add some red food coloring to the water in the tank. Come back in about an hour and see if the water in the bowl is pink. If it is, your flapper probably needs to be replaced.

   Showers

Cleaning your showerhead.

Did you know that a bug called atypical mycobacteria can build up on a shower head which can cause coughing and shortness of breath and be especially dangerous for COPD sufferers? Every six months, fill a plastic bag with white vinegar and attach it to the shower head with a rubber band so the head is submerged. Let it soak overnight. In the morning, remove the bag and run the shower to rinse. This process will remove calcium deposits as well as any lingering bacteria.

Clean your shower drain.

Keep the clogs at bay by regularly cleaning your shower drain. Just pour a pot of very hot water (NOT boiling) down the drain, add ½ cup baking soda and let it sit for a few minutes. Then, combine one cup of vinegar and one cup of very hot water and pour into the drain. Cover with a wet cloth or drain plug and let it sit for 10 minutes. Uncover and pour another pot of very hot water (NOT boiling) down the drain. This should keep your shower drain running freely. Note: Boiling water can harm plastic pipes!

Avoid soap build up on glass shower doors.

Apply a thin coat of car wax to the doors. Let dry. Buff doors. Make sure wax doesn't get on the shower floor (it's very slippery!).

Water Heaters

New water heater standards in U.S.A.

In 2015 sweeping changes that affect the entire water heater industry went into law. These new federally mandated requirements call for higher energy factor (EF) ratings on virtually all residential gas, electric, oil and tankless gas water heaters. What does this mean for the average consumer? Water heaters will be larger, more complex and more expensive. Why? Because in order to meet the higher energy factor ratings, they will require more insulation, use newer flue baffling technologies, use electronic ignition in lieu of the standing pilot or any combination of these. Many water heaters are placed in "tight" quarters and since they will be larger, changes may have to be made to accommodate the larger heater or owners will have to go to a lower capacity water heater to fit in the current space. The new water heaters are at least 2" taller and 2" wider. It is estimated that the average homeowner will save $365 per year with the new style water heaters.

How long does a water heater last?

Three factors contribute to the life expectancy of a water heater – water quality, water pressure and maintenance. Homeowners with well water should be very concerned about the water quality but not pressure (extreme pressures spikes are rare with well systems). Public water supply systems should always supply water that is safe to drink, but may not be safe for your water heater and other appliances (mainly because of water hardness). Water pressure can fluctuate drastically with public water supply, especially at night.

Don't get burned!

Tub and shower valves should be set at no more than 120 degrees. Most modern single handle tub/shower valves have integral temperature limit components. These devices basically limit how far the handle will turn towards the hot side of the faucet. Soaking/whirlpool tubs will almost always have two handle faucets. The temperature at these faucets should be limited by means of a mixing valve. The mixing valve will be installed in a remote location, usually through an access panel in a closet or vanity cabinet.

How do you know if your water heater is on the fritz?

- Look for drips, leaks or accumulated water underneath.
- Check out the flame if you use a gas water heater – the light should burn mostly blue, not yellow.
- Is the water in your shower too hot, too cold or not reflecting the temperature to which the dial is set?
- Rust coming out of the faucet is a big red flag as well as any bending or cracking in the water heater tank.

Water heaters need tender loving care too.

Water heater maintenance is easy to overlook because the tank just sits there and has no moving parts to worry about. But inside, two things are constantly attacking your water heater: sediment and rust. To keep your water heater operating correctly, your water heater needs regular maintenance to minimize rust and calcium carbonate. This should be done by an experienced and licensed plumber. However, there is one easy thing that you can do throughout the year – check around the base of your water heater for evidence of leaks. If your water is hard and your water heater is over 5 years old, it should be checked monthly for leaks or rust at the bottom. If water leakage or rust is found, the water heater should be replaced. Regular annual maintenance will definitely enhance the operation of your water heater & help you save money.

Water Conditioning

Why should I test my water?

Whether your water comes from private wells or municipal utilities, it can have any number of chemicals that may affect its quality, taste or smell. Plus scale from hard water builds up in your faucets, dishwasher, coffee maker and other appliances. Your water can be treated for iron, hardness, sediments, bacteria, chlorine and arsenic.

The presence of pathogens and chemicals in our drinking water can lead to health problems, including gastrointestinal illness, reproductive problems and neurological disorders. Infants, young children, pregnant women, the elderly and people whose immune systems are compromised because of AIDS, chemotherapy or transplant medications may be especially susceptible to illness from certain contaminants.

Causes for water contamination.

- Septic Tanks
- Fertilization & Pesticides
- Industrial Pollutants & Waste
- Landfills & Dumps
- Household Water
- Leaking Underground Tanks and Piping
- Sources from Nature (Arsenic)
- Lead Poisoning
- Radon

Lead in your pipes.

Many homes (especially in older cities) still have lead service lines connected to galvanized pipes (in your home) which may contribute lead to residential drinking water. Not only does the lead service line release lead into the water but the galvanized pipes within your home release lead and iron into your drinking water too. Older inside fixtures (faucets, etc.) can also be a source of lead. The only way to fully ensure that lead is not being released from galvanized plumbing lines is the complete replacement of your galvanized piping. If you can't do that, then you can certainly add a certified filter that can remove lead at the tap.

What is hard water?

Did you know that 85% of the country has hard water! Hard water is a result of the dissolved minerals calcium, magnesium and manganese. When these minerals are present you will see the following:

- Soap scum in sinks and rings in bathtubs.
- Spots on dishes or shower doors.
- Reduced foaming and cleaning abilities of soaps and detergents.
- Dingy and yellowed clothes with soapy residues that require extra rinsing to remove.
- Clogged pipes from buildup of minerals.
- Increased water heating costs from buildup of minerals, reducing efficiency of water heaters.

If you suspect that you have hard water, it can be tested. If you are connected to a public supply, call your water superintendent and ask if the water is hard. If you are on a private supply, have your water tested by an approved testing lab. Water is considered hard when it exceeds 3 grains per gallon (GPG).

If your water turns out to be above 3 grains per gallon, it is time to research what water softening options are available to you. The most common way to soften water is through an ion exchange water softener. This system works by exchanging positively charged hardness minerals (calcium and magnesium) with positively charged softness minerals (sodium or potassium) on a resin surface that is regenerated. This exchange of minerals softens the water and can extend the life of plumbing systems since there is reduced clogging in the pipes.

What kind of testing should I do?

First of all, your water should be tested annually. Keep the records so you can see if anything changes over the years. Many in-home tests are available and are accurate. In many areas there are local non-profit watershed groups that might also provide testing and of course, there are professional certified labs that provide testing. At the very least, you should test for hardness and bacteria. And, depending on your geographic area, consider testing for radon, arsenic and pesticides.

Once your own water situation is analyzed, there are many solutions for your water issues – whether its iron, lead, arsenic, hard water, sediments, bacterial or chlorine, there is water conditioning equipment to take care of the problem. Reach out to a plumbing or water conditioning professional. Permits may be required for installation of such equipment in some municipalities.

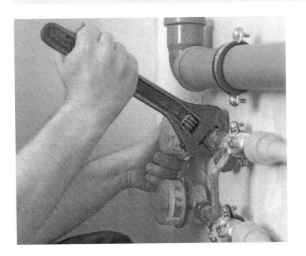

Water Piping
Outside hose bibs (spigot).

Keep your outside pipes from freezing! Remove all the garden hoses from the hose bibs (including from frost free hose bibs). If you don't have frost free hose bibs, consider having them installed. If you have the traditional hose bib, it must be shut off inside and drained in order to ensure freezing doesn't occur.

Sump Pumps
Types of sump pumps.

Sump pumps are electrical pumps that are usually located in your basement to drain water out in case of flooding. Generally speaking there are two different kinds of sump pumps. The pedestal style and the submersible. The pedestal style pump sits in an upright position on top of the sump pit and the submersible pump is just that – submersed down inside the sump pit. For either style pump, you should make regular inspections to ensure it is working properly (especially before the rainy season begins). For extra protection a battery backup system is recommended for sump pumps. And, remember, the sump pump should discharge as far away from the house as possible to keep the foundation as dry as possible.

Water Meters

This is the device that measures the amount of water your home uses and how your water bill is calculated. They may be installed outside in a pit with a metal lid, but most commonly, they are located in the lowest level of your home. They should have a valve on either side for servicing. You should inspect twice a year for any leaks and contact your water supplier if any leaks are observed.

42

Septic Systems

Fundamentals.

If you have a septic system serving your home for wastewater, it is your responsibility to maintain it. By maintaining it regularly you will protect your investment in your entire home.

According to the EPA the average household septic system should be inspected at least every three years by a septic service professional. Household tanks are usually pumped out every three to five years but that really depends on household size, total wastewater generated, volume of solids in the wastewater and the size of the septic tank. Always check with your local municipality or health department regarding septic systems.

Keep in mind that if you have a septic system, all water goes through it, so even a small leak or running toilet can waste hundreds of gallons of water a day and puts more stress on your septic system. And, remember toilets are not trash cans. Never flush anything besides human waste and toilet paper down your toilet to a septic field.

Basically, your septic system is a collection of living organisms that digest and treat household waste in your septic tank. Therefore, avoid pouring any of these items into it: chemical drain openers (use hot – not boiling - water or drain snake), cooking oil or grease, oil-based paints, solvents, even latex paint should be minimized. Also, eliminate or limit the use of a garbage disposal.

Other tips for longevity include never parking or driving on top of your septic field, don't plant trees on top of your field and keep roof drains, sump pumps and other rainwater drainage systems away from your septic field.

Backflow Preventers

What is a Backflow Preventer?

A backflow prevention device is used to protect water supplies from contamination or pollution. Public and private drinking water is at risk without proper backflow devices and periodic inspections.

There are many types of backflows for the various levels of hazard for both residential and commercial use. Your local water company and local municipal plumbing official can assist you with what you need to know for your home.

44

5 HEATING & AIR CONDITIONING

Energy Savings = $$$

Did you know that as much as half of the energy used in your home goes to heating and cooling? Making smart decisions about your home's heating, ventilating, and air conditioning (HVAC) system can have a big effect on your utility bills, your comfort and most importantly, your health. With today's technology, the heating and air conditioning industry is continually developing new products that are more energy efficient and safe. If your furnace or air conditioner is more than 15 years old, start doing your research now!

Air Quality

As you can imagine, there's a lot about indoor air quality that you might not know and you certainly can't see. It is estimated that up to 72 trillion microscopic irritants, or allergens, find their way into your home every day --dust, pollen, pet hair and dander, dust mites, mildew, lint, fungus, tobacco smoke, cooking grease and bacteria. Many of these particles are so small that your nose and throat can't filter them out, and they can get deep into you.

Most people assume their indoor air is pretty clean. Actually, studies show that indoor air can be five times more polluted than outdoor air. Exposure to indoor air pollutants has increased in recent years because today's homes are better insulated and more tightly sealed than ever before, sealing in humidity, smoke, dust and other pollutants.

All furnace and air conditioning systems are equipped with air filters which REALLY SHOULD BE CHANGED MONTHLY. Quarterly is a really good idea. At least do it once per year. If you have animals with a lot of fur in your home, monthly is probably better. You can purchase filters in bulk and just keep them on hand. Remember, it is actually safer to run the HVAC system (temporarily) with NO filter than to run it with a very clogged filter. For anyone seeking relief from allergies or asthma, you might consider a whole-house air-cleaning system. They are becoming increasingly more popular and can be incorporated into almost any heating and air conditioning system. Whole house purification systems can work 100 times more effectively than conventional furnace filter systems. They also don't add any noise (like a portable unit).

DISASTER ZONE

It wasn't just years of debris and dust building up in Susan and Will's furnace. Because they had neglected the annual fall furnace tune-up, many cracks had formed in the combustion chamber. Thankfully, they had placed a carbon monoxide detector near the furnace and were alerted when the gases were leaking into the home, saving their lives.

Furnace and Air Conditioning

Pay attention to your furnace and air conditioning units.

Every fall and spring have a professional heating/air conditioning contractor inspect and maintain your systems as recommended by the manufacturer.

Maintenance should include: cleaning, lubricating fans and motors, tightening or changing belts, checking electrical safeties, drain pan for leaks, condensate drain, testing the capacitors, calibrating the thermostat.

Here are also some things you can maintain throughout the year and save money.

- Install a programmable thermostat. It is estimated you can save about $180 per year in energy costs.
- Change your AC filter at least every 3 months (or more depending on how heavily you are using your air conditioner).
- Consider having your ducts cleaned by a professional cleaning company.
- Check the condensate hose to be sure it is not blocked with algae.
- Clean the outside condensing unit screen of leaves.
- Always listen for unusual noises.

If you are unsure how to perform any of these tasks, ask your contractor to show you how to perform these maintenance items when they are there performing your fall and spring tune ups.

Air Conditioners

Every air conditioner unit should have a drain pan. Take a look at your pan to make sure it is draining freely. If there is standing water where your condensation line drains, create a drainage path using a small garden trowel and line the path with gravel. Always keep the screen around your unit free from leaves and debris to keep the air flowing through it too.

Humidity

The relative humidity in your home should be between 30% and 50% (with 40% about ideal). Too much humidity and too little humidity both can have negative side affects. Too much humidity causes mold and fungus and too little humidity causes air dryness which isn't good for your sinuses. Stagnant air is humidity's best friend so check all the areas in your home where air does NOT circulate —behind curtains, under beds, and in closets. You are looking for dampness and mildew. When you see condensation on windows or wet stains on walls and ceilings or have musty smells, these are all signs that you have too much humidity in your home. Tell your family to always use the bathroom exhaust fan when showering to help move the humid air out of the room. Never turn the air conditioner off when you leave on a trip; only turn it up. If you are concerned at all about the humidity level in your home, consult with a mechanical contractor or air conditioning repair company to determine if your HVAC system is properly sized and in good working order.

Ceiling Fans

Most ceiling fans have two modes. Set it to blow down on you in the summer (counter clockwise) and change the switch to pull air upwards and away from you during the winter.

TYPES OF HEATING & COOLING SYSTEMS
CENTRAL HEATING SYSTEMS

Furnace

The majority of households in America depend on a central furnace to provide their heat. The furnace blows heated air into a duct system throughout the house. This is called a duct-warmed or forced warm-air distribution system. These systems can be powered by electricity, natural gas or fuel oil.

Boiler

Boilers are really special purpose water heaters. A boiler system distributes its heat through heating the water and passing it through radiators throughout the home. Hot water systems can also be called hydronic. A boiler system uses natural gas or fuel oil for its energy source.

Heat Pump

Heat pumps move heat from one place to another. Even if air is cold, heat energy is present. The heat pump extracts that heat and moves it into the home. The opposite is true for warm weather; the heat pump actually reverses the process to push the unwanted heat to the outside to cool the inside. Heat pumps are ideal for moderate climates. In colder climates, electric powered heat pumps can serve as a great combination with your oil-fired or gas-fueled furnace.

CENTRAL COOLING SYSTEMS

Central Air Conditioner & Heat Pump

Instead of using energy to create heat, air conditioners and heat pumps use energy to take heat away. The most common air conditioning system uses a compressor much like your refrigerator. The compressor transfers heat from your house to the outdoors. Central air conditioning systems are designed to cool your entire house.

Air conditioners are rated according to their "seasonal energy efficiency ratio", otherwise known as their SEER rating. SEER is the seasonal cooling output in Btu divided by the seasonal energy input in watt-hours for an "average" U.S. climate. The higher the unit's SEER rating the more energy efficient it is. The national efficiency standard for central air conditioners and air source heat pumps now requires a minimum SEER of 13 (since 2006), and to qualify for ENERGY STAR requires a SEER of 14.5 or higher.

Ductless Mini-split Heating and Air Conditioners

Mini-split heating and air conditioners are very popular in other countries. Here in the U.S. they are an excellent option for room additions or houses without ductwork already in place. Like a conventional hvac system, mini-splits use an outside compressor/condenser and indoor air handling units. Each room or zone is cooled by its own air handler unit. Each indoor unit is connected to the outdoor unit by a conduit that carries the power and refrigerant lines. Indoor units are typically mounted on the wall or ceiling.

When it comes to the exterior of your home, water is your biggest enemy. Roofs, siding, gutters, and vents are all areas for water to infiltrate. Water is bad when it comes to your home. You want to keep it out in any way. Periodic checks of your roof, gutters, attic, vents, siding, windows, doors, foundation and interior walls will help keep your overall costs down by catching a problem before it becomes a disaster.

A roof is a roof is a roof. Not really! The performance of your roof is so important to the overall well being of your home. Remember, WATER is bad!!! All the components of your roofing system need to be working to keep the water out.

Roof Components

- Sheathing – Plywood over the rafters.

- Underlayment – Tar paper or roofing membrane laid over the plywood prior to the shingles.

- Ice & Water Shield – A rubberized self-sealing membrane applied at the bottom of the roof line intended to prevent ice damming.

- Flashing – Metal pieces used to divert water from areas where it might collect (hips and valleys) and prevent it from infiltrating your house.

- Shingles – Outermost part of the roof. Can be a variety of materials including wood, stone, concrete or metal. There are other types of roofs but these are the most common on houses.

- Pipe Flanges – Typically, made from metal and/or plastic to prevent leakage around plumbing and exhaust vent pipes. The rubber can typically crack and deteriorate due to the UV rays from the sun and should be inspected periodically. They typically do not last as long as the roof itself.

Roof Design Elements

- Pitch – Slope or steepness of roof.
- Ridge – Highest peak on roof.
- Hip – Highest point where two adjoining roof sections meet.
- Valley – When two roof sections slope down and meet, they create a "valley."
- Eaves – The part of the roof that extends over the walls of the home.
- Gable – Triangular section of the ends of the home, which go from the eaves to the peak of roof.
- Dormer – Sections of the roof that extend from the roof and typically have windows to get light into the home or attic.

Ice Damming

Ice damming occurs when snow and ice build up over the eaves of your roof creating a "dam" of ice. When the dam starts to melt, water backs up underneath shingles and into your house. Proper roof ventilation, adequate attic insulation and the installation of ice and water shield along the lower 4'-6' of the roof line will minimize the chances of ice damming.

Attics

Attics should be similar in temperature to the exterior temperature. Therefore, the most important thing about your attic is to be adequately insulated. Air or heat loss from your living space into your attic can cause ice damming, especially if your attic is poorly ventilated. Check and make sure the insulation covers all areas and is secure and adequate. A minimum of an R-38 value is recommended when possible. To look for leaks check the bottom side of the roof sheathing, roof rafters/trusses, and around any vent pipes or roof vents for water stains.

Checking For Roof Leaks

Your roof should be inspected periodically for damage (especially after any big storm). The weird thing about roof leaks is that they can be hard to trace because the water may run along the attic floor, rafters, or truss for quite a distance before coming through the ceiling.

You will need to both look and touch the wood to determine if you have any rotting wood. Sometimes it is in plain sight and other times it hides behind cracked paint or under siding. Use a screwdriver and flashlight to take a good look and get a good feel. Just remember this: wood should NOT be soft to the touch.

Damaged shingles should be replaced quickly. The longer you wait, the more water infiltrates and spreads throughout that area. Pay special attention to shingles around skylights, vents and chimneys. These areas are the most leak-prone.

Gutters

Gutters play a very important role in keeping your house dry. They are your main line of defense for your foundation and siding against the elements. They are designed to capture water and debris and move it all away from your foundation and siding. One of the main causes of water in basements is the lack of gutter cleaning and maintenance by homeowners.

Clean your gutters at least once per year, if not more often. Remove the leaves and use your garden hose to make sure the downspouts are clear. Install splash blocks on the ground in front of the downspouts so water is moved further away from your house. Also, check that the gutters are tightly secured to the fascia boards (flat surface of wood above).

I can not stress enough that gutters and extensions should route water AWAY from your house. Remember, 10 minutes plus $10 can save $10,000.00!

⚠ DISASTER ZONE ⚠

Maria and Pat's roof was badly damaged in a Nor'easter so they hired a contractor to repair it. The crew fixed the roof, got paid and went on their way. Unbelievably, two months after the repair, they got hit again in another huge storm. With part of the roof missing, they discovered that the prior contractor had not installed ice and water shield (like they were supposed to). The entire roof had to be done again.

Vents

Take a look at your roof and you will see multiple vents (all possible sources of leaks). There will be gable vents, attic vents, exhaust vents, plumbing vents, clothes dryer vents. All vents should exhaust to the exterior, be in good working order and have proper pipe flanges.

Decking

Most older decks are made of wood (cedar, treated lumber, hardwoods). Today you have a myriad of options with man made decking materials (which require almost no maintenance).

If you do have a wooden deck though, make sure and check for rotting or loose boards. Replace as soon as possible and re-stain. Check all the railings and steps too. If any of those are loose or rotting, of course, get them replaced as soon as possible.

And, don't forget your ledger board! What is that? Look for the piece of wood that attaches your deck to the house. It is called the ledger board and it should be properly flashed. If that is not the case, water can get behind it, eventually causing water damage to your house. This is a very important inspection to make because if there is rot behind your ledger board, it can spread to the home's structure under the siding.

Siding Components

Siding can be made of wood, metal, vinyl, masonry or composite materials. It is the exterior portion of the house that keeps water from entering the structure. Under the siding there will be a vapor barrier such as Tyvec (house wrap or felt paper), which is installed on top of the exterior wood sheathing.

Flashing

You might notice a thin metal strip above your doors and windows, under your thresholds, and around your chimneys, or other components of your house. This is called "flashing" and is designed to prevent water from getting into spaces where two different building surfaces meet. If done improperly, and this happens often, this can lead to significant water damage to your house. The lack of a small piece of flashing or improperly installed flashing can cause significant damage if it goes unnoticed for a long time.

Inspect your siding and trim regularly. Any siding or trim that appears to have water damage should be replaced and the source investigated. This could be a sign of a much more serious problem. Also, the exterior sided wall of a wooden framed house should have at least 8" between the wood and the surrounding soil.

7

WINDOWS, SKYLIGHTS, FLOORS & DOORS

Windows, skylights, floors and doors are certainly a source for water and air leaks. You can save as much as 15% on your heating bill by making sure these building components are sealed. Check for leaks especially near the corners. Check for peeling paint, it can be a sign of water getting into the wood. Look for discolorations in paint or caulking and/or swelling of the window or doorframe or surrounding materials. These are all signs of water infiltration.

Leaky Windows

Depending on the siding (because if it is vinyl there is no caulking), it is advisable to check the caulk around your windows to ensure there are no places for water infiltration. If the caulk is dry, cracked or weathered, remove the old caulk with a box cutter or other sharp knife and run a new bead (line) of caulk along the seam. For even more savings on your energy bills, try applying an insulating window film over the glass.

Sweaty Windows

Condensation on some windows is not uncommon especially single-pane glass windows or even thermal pane windows in extreme cold situations. Excessive condensation can contribute to the growth of mold or mildew in or on the walls. It can also damage the paint surface and eventually rot the wood. The simplest and most effective way to control condensation is by reducing interior humidity. Use vent fans (in kitchens and bathrooms). Use a dehumidifier to lower interior humidity levels.

Foggy Windows.

Thermal pane windows are vacuum sealed. If that seal breaks, moisture can enter between the panes of glass. This will cause a fogging of the window that cannot be washed off and can only be repaired by a glass specialist, who would replace the pane of glass.

///// DISASTER ZONE /////

On a particularly rainy spring day, Rosanne noticed that there was water dripping down the inside of the windows in her kitchen. She wiped the water off the window and chalked it up to the heavy rain. The next week, she looked up and saw that some of the paint around the window was coming off the wall. Rosanne called a professional and ended up replacing the leaky windows.

Skylights

Skylights come in numerous styles from fixed to venting units. Most newer units are thermal pane. Since they are on the roof it is not uncommon for condensation to build up on the glass and cause staining on the frames at the lower corners. This is not a significant concern, however, if staining is significant and/or the skylights are very old, they could be leaking. The glass on thermal skylights can fog just as they can on windows.

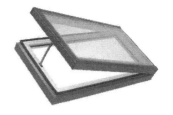

Sagging Floors

It is not uncommon for floors to develop some amount of sag in them over time. This is called deflection and if within tolerance, is not a significant problem. However, sagging floors could also be an indication of undersized floor joists or trusses or improper spacing. It could also be an indication of damage from water or insect infiltration.

Stuck Sliding Windows/Doors

In older homes windows and doors may swell due to humidity which could cause them to stick or bind. This can often be corrected by a carpenter who can adjust them properly. For newer windows, spray a little silicone spray lubricant onto a rag and wipe along the window tracks and and/or the hardware. This may help unstick them and operate more freely.

Squeaky Door Hinges

Spray a little WD-40 onto the hinges and move the door back and forth to work in the lubricant. You can also use petroleum jelly to lubricate the hinges (but the hinge pin needs to be removed in order to do this properly).

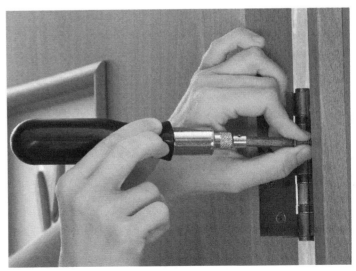

TYPES OF WINDOWS

Windows are for light, decoration and air flow. They can be square, round, rectangular and any myriad of shapes and sizes. Some windows open at the side, some at the top and even some at the bottom. They can be single hung (only the bottom portion of window opens while the top part stays stationary) or they can be double hung (both top and bottom windows can open). Knowing about all the different types of windows will help you decide what works best for your situation.

Arched Windows

These windows add architectural complexity to a home's design. They are mostly for aesthetics and used above standard windows and doors.

Awning Windows

These windows are hinged at the top and open outward. They can also be placed alongside other stationary windows on a home.

Bay or Bow Windows

You can combine all kinds of windows in a bay/ bow window set up. Stationary in the middle with double hung or casements on the side for air flow. They also give you more interior space.

Casement Windows

Turn the crank on a casement window to open them either left or right or outward.

Glass Block Windows

A great choice when you want to add accents but also bring light into a space. Glass block windows also add a great deal of privacy too.

Picture Window

A large stationary window, usually with a view to the outdoors. They are designed to capture the maximum amount of light and view.

Egress Windows

Egress windows are installed for safety more than anything else. They are typically installed in your basement so that anyone can climb out of them in an emergency.

Garden Windows

Think of a garden window as a mini-bay window meant for plants. You can install them almost anywhere. The plants that you can grow in these windows will add a lot of life to your home.

Jalousie Windows

The Jalousie window was common years ago because they were easy to maintain and were affordable. Basically, they operated like a set of blinds. Crank a lever and the glass slats tilt to let air flow through.

Hopper Windows

Commonly used in basements, hopper windows open from the top and usually crank open to tip down into the room, basement or other building type. They offer great ventilation and make good use of compact spaces.

Round Windows

The round window category includes round, half round, elliptical or oval. These windows add architectural detail and also are used to enhance structures from certain historical periods like the Victorian or Gothic eras.

Skylights

When you need light in the middle of your home install a skylight. They are installed similar to a roof vent (so no roof leaks happen). Some skylights open and close but most are stationary.

Slider Windows

Slider windows usually open to a deck or back yard. One window is stationary and the other glides on the track.

Stationary Windows

Stationary windows do not open but they can be customized to any shape and are typically used in modern home designs.

Storm Windows

If your windows are old and letting in cold air, install storm windows. Studies show that you can get nearly the same results as new windows if you install storm windows where appropriate.

Transom Window

Designed to let either light or air into a space, a transom window is narrow and usually placed above a door or another window. It can be stationary or open up.

8

FOUNDATIONS & BASEMENTS

Foundations can be made of stone, block or poured concrete. Typically, much older homes have stone foundations. Newer homes usually have block or poured concrete foundations. Poured concrete foundations are essentially waterproof due to their density, unless they crack. If these cracks leak, they can be repaired by a professional. Block and stone foundations can not be repaired in this manner.

If you find water infiltration, first identify the source and location of the leak. If it is from a crack, it may be possible to seal the crack. If the leak is coming through the walls or floor, the first plan of attack should always be to minimize or eliminate the source of water infiltration. (Such as improper grading or gutter discharge at house foundation or clogged overflowing gutters.) If all measures are taken and water still infiltrates your basement, the installation of a perimeter drain may be required.

All types of foundations can heave, settle, flood and allow water and radon to enter the basement. It is important that inspections be made around the interior of your basement and the exterior of your foundation on a regular basis.

How to Spot Water Infiltration

Inside the house look for:

- Stains.
- Mold.
- Standing water.
- Cracks and holes in joints.

Check all locations where piping or wiring come into the house.

Outside around the foundation you should:

- Check your gutters and downspouts to make sure they are diverting water away from the foundation adequately and far enough.

- After a rain go outside and look for any puddles within 10 feet of the foundation. If you see them, fill in the low spots with rock or soil so that water keeps draining away from the foundation instead of standing next to the foundation.

- Ensure the grading around your house slopes away from your foundation.

////// DISASTER ZONE //////

As she went down the stairs of the basement, Lois noticed that a crack in the concrete wall had extended a few inches. Her husband Lyle had marked the end point several months earlier so it was clear the crack was growing. They called in a professional and were able to determine that the vertical crack needed to be filled to prevent further spreading.

Unfinished Basements

If you have an unfinished basement, take some masking tape and cover any cracks you see and write today's date on them. In a few months, check the tape again. If you see the crack growing out of the end of the tape, you might have a problem.

Foundation and Exterior

Seal any cracks and holes in external walls, joints, and foundations. In particular, examine locations where piping or wiring extends through the outside walls. Fill all cracks in these locations with a masonry sealant or mortar. The joints may need to be cut out more in order to properly fill with mortar.

Basement Waterproofing

If you have water in your basement from cracks in floors or walls, you might need to look at basement waterproofing contractors. As mentioned many times before, water is BAD for your home. Before you think about spending thousands of dollars on basement waterproofing make sure you have done your research. There are a variety of choices and approaches in basement waterproofing repairs or systems. They are all designed to tackle the problem, but, as with many things, there are different opinions about which one is the most effective.

The majority of basement problems are a combination of events. Therefore, the repairs or installation of a waterproofing system can vary widely. Regardless of what you choose, first make sure all the exterior problems have been taken care of - check out your home's gutters, downspouts or other drainage systems that are in place. Make sure they are working effectively and diverting water away from the home. Also, check the grade of soil around the foundation. It should slope away from the house to encourage water to flow away from exterior walls, not toward them. Here are some of the types of basement waterproofing solutions.

Waterproofing primer or paint products.

Most contractors agree that waterproofing paints or primers have limited sealing ability and are little more than a cosmetic solution, especially if the water source problem isn't addressed.

Crack injections.

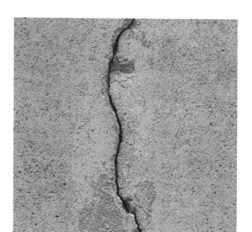

Crack injections are only suitable for poured concrete foundations where seepage is coming from the walls and not the floors. You can't really use the crack injection method on foundations that are made of stone, brick or cinder block. Injecting the epoxy material into a crack can help prevent water from entering the basement, but many regard this as temporary fix and not a permanent solution.

Exterior excavation waterproofing.

This is usually the most expensive but also the most effective way to stop water from entering your basement. It is an especially good choice if the home is situated in a high water table area. This method involves excavating 6 to 8 feet down to the foundation wall footer and correcting drainage by installing new drainage tiles or a French drain system. In addition to the drain, waterproofing companies will also typically apply a waterproof material or membrane to the exterior wall's surface to make sure that water doesn't infiltrate it again. Considerations include cost, disruption to landscaping, porches, driveways, etc.

Interior excavation waterproofing.

Interior waterproofing methods cost less and are less invasive. A contractor will basically jackhammer the perimeter of your interior basement to install a new drainage and sump pump system. Along with the installation of a sump pump, a backup battery sump pump should also be installed (for use during power outages). Obviously, if the basement is already finished, this method can be pretty invasive, but if your basement is not finished, it is a much easier installation.

62

9 PAINT & TILE

Lead Based Paint: Rules & Testing

Lead paint is still in many homes and businesses. If it is disturbed, the lead dust can create hazardous conditions for humans. If your home was built before 1978, lead paint may have been used on some or all of the surfaces. If you are concerned, you can purchase a lead test kit from a paint supply store and follow the instructions accordingly. Or, have a contractor test the areas of concern. If excessive amounts of lead are found, you may want to contact a certified lead abatement contractor. If a contractor is going to work in your home and disturb any lead painted areas, make sure your contractor is Lead Safe Certified by the EPA and meets any other state requirements.

What kind of paint should I use?

Most interior and exterior paints used today are latex and are very durable. Oil based paints are still available but used less commonly due to VOC (volatile organic compound) compliance issues. Since bathrooms can have condensation build up from showers, etc., it is recommended to paint the walls and ceilings with a proper bathroom paint. Your paint supplier should be able to assist you with this. In general, walls and ceilings are painted with either a flat or matte finish. Trim is typically satin, semi-gloss or high gloss paint, depending on your preference. Matte paints are easier to clean than flat paints. Higher sheen paints will show off any imperfections more so than flat paints (nail pops, tape joints, etc.).

▟▟▟ DISASTER ZONE ▟▟▟

Peter and Leslie wanted to renovate their laundry room and picked out a beautiful Moroccan tile for the floors. The contractor insisted that the tile would look better without grout, so they continued the installation. Soon after the renovation was complete, the expensive tile started cracking into shards. Peter and Leslie had to hire another contractor to install a cheaper tile since they had already blown their budget the ruined Moroccan tile.

Drywall

Before you start any painting project, you should take a good look at your drywall and repair any nail pops, dings or cracks and spot prime any repairs. If you see signs of mold or staining on your drywall, that could be an indication of water damage. The source of those stains should be located and repaired as necessary prior to painting those areas. If the staining is minimal, an oil based primer can be applied prior to applying finish coats of paint. If the damage is significant, that area of drywall should be replaced.

Spackling
You can easily handle small spackle jobs!
Take your time and follow these tips.

1. Choose the right spackle/joint compound. For small holes a light weight spackle will be all you need. For cracks and larger holes, you may need to tape and apply joint compound prior to painting.

2. Using a utility knife, cut out the bad area (don't make hole any bigger than you have to, but make sure it is a clean cut all around).

3. If you are filling nail pops, don't cut out around them, just gently tap a nail punch with a hammer, wipe away any crumbling drywall and follow #4 below. If you discover a screw instead of a nail, just tighten the screw and then follow #4.

4. Use a spackle knife that is a little bigger than the hole. Load the knife with spackle and press the loaded side into the wall starting about a half an inch above the hole. Press down hard, and pull the knife down over the hole. Sometimes it takes a couple of coats. Don't apply the 2nd coat until the first coat is fully dry. This is where the patience comes in.

5. Remember that spackle will shrink so don't be afraid to leave a small mound of spackle above the hole. After it is dry you can use very fine sand paper or a damp sponge to smooth out the surface. You want the repair to be flush with the wall.

6. Use a latex primer paint before you apply finish paint unless the area has been stained. An oil based primer would be needed to seal the water stain. Water stains will bleed through a latex primer.

Matching Paint Color

From a clean area of the wall and with a utility knife, cut out a 2" x 2" section of the drywall face (about 1/8" deep). Take to your local paint store for matching. You can try touching up the wall with the matched paint, but due to either age, sheen or the paint not being an exact match, the touched up area may stand out. More than likely you will need to paint from corner to corner of the wall. When you do that the paint color discrepancy will not be as noticeable.

Painting Over Water Damage

I can't tell you how many times I've heard someone say that they painted over some old water damage and then the stain came back. They always want to know if the leak is back too? The answer is "not necessarily." Before painting, water stains MUST be primed with an oil based stain blocker. Latex primers and paints will let the stain bleed through over time.

DISASTER ZONE

Rachel and Kevin hired a contractor and asked him to redo their popcorn ceiling with a lightly textured finish. Unbeknownst to them, their contractor hired a subcontractor, and he applied that texture to every wall, ceiling and surface and in the kitchen. All of it had to be scraped down, sanded and smoothed out. It set their kitchen remodel back weeks. They didn't have a written contract and only had one phone number for the contractor. He wouldn't return their calls. They ended up paying to have the mistake corrected.

Exterior Painting Tips

Painted Exterior Trim

All exterior wood trim or paneling should be sealed or painted on all sides and edges prior to installation to prevent water absorption. An alternative to wood trim is PVC composite or urethane trim. If wood is desired, cedar makes a better choice than pine, as it is more resistant to insect and water damage.

Why does your house paint peel?

Exterior paint typically peels due to moisture being absorbed into the wood and then trying to escape, which pushes the paint off of the wood. This can happen when people are in a hurry and don't realize that they need to wait at least a few days after powerwashing a house to begin painting it. The siding and/or trim must be dry. This can be tested with a moisture meter. Remember, wood trim should be painted on all sides and ends prior to installation. This is often overlooked by contractors as it is very time consuming and expensive. Stained wood siding typically holds up better than paint. Painted wood siding is not uncommon but is typically a higher maintenance way to go.

Ewww…Mildew

Another problem with exterior paint is mildew. You have basically two options to clean mildew. Use a commercial siding cleaner or mix one part bleach to three parts water. Sponge or mop on and leave for 20 minutes, then rinse thoroughly. Always wear eye and hand protection when applying this mix! And, remember if you use bleach, be careful not to get the water around your plants, they will die if they get too much bleached water.

Paint Disposal

If you only have a small amount of paint left, just brush the leftover paint on cardboard or newspaper to use it up. Let the empty paint can dry with the lid off before disposal. For larger quantities, you can mix latex paint with kitty litter and put in the regular trash. Oil based paint is considered hazardous material and should be treated as such. Contact your local municipality for their regulations about disposing of oil based paint. Many municipalities have "hazardous waste" days for collection of such materials.

Tile & Stone on Walls, Floors & Backsplashes

There are so many options in tile and stone today – both real and faux. One thing is for certain though, we all want our tile or stone floors, walls and backsplashes to look clean and fresh. Before any tile floor, wall or backsplash can be completed, you will need to know more about the construction of your floors and walls, which will dictate how it is prepared for tile or stone.

Floors

Subfloor

Subfloors can be made from numerous different products depending on the age of the house. Older homes may have tongue and groove flooring while newer homes may have plywood subflooring. The thickness of the subflooring can vary from a ½" to ¾" or more.

Underlayment

There should be a layer of underlayment between the subfloor and the tile. Typically, the underlayment would either be cement board, uncoupling membrane or plywood. Cement board and uncoupling membranes are preferable due to their resistance to water. But, in any case, the flooring should be of proper thickness, typically 1 ¼". However, this can vary based on joist size and spacing.

Slab

You can typically tile directly over a slab floor as long as it is clean. If it has cracks or there are concerns of cracking, installation of a crack isolation membrane between the tile and the slab will minimize the chance of the tiles cracking.

Walls/Backsplashes

Tile or stone can be installed directly over primed drywall for areas that will not get very wet such as for a backsplash in a kitchen. However, if tiling a shower or tub wall, the installation of a cement board or waterproof backer board in the tub/shower area is recommended. Years ago it was very common for tile to be applied right over drywall in showers and around bathtubs. This was before the availability of these new water proofing products to stop water infiltration. There are still a lot of bathrooms with tile installed directly on drywall and over time water can get through cracks, or just penetrate through grout and deteriorate the drywall.

Grout & Caulk

It is important to know the difference between grout and caulk because these two products are designed for different uses in your home. Also, it is important to know that different adhesive products respond to heat, humidity and cold in different ways. Using the right product for the right job will always have a better result.

Grout

Used for ceramic tile and stone. Comes in different color hues and when it dries it is not flexible. Grout can be sealed with a topical grout sealer (spray or sponge on). Or, grout can be mixed with a sealer in place of water before applying the grout to the tile or stone. The latter being more effective at stain resistance.

If grout cracks or fails, it can be removed and new grout can be installed. However, this could be a minor issue or could be an indication of tiles coming loose; especially if they are floor tiles. If the tiles are coming loose, re-grouting will not solve the problem, the loose tiles must be repaired or secured.

Caulk

Used for filling the gaps between different types of products (tile, tub, floor). Very flexible sealant. Comes in tubes and is applied with a caulk "gun". However, caulk can be purchased in smaller tubes that can be applied without the gun (especially good for a beginner). Caulk also comes in a variety of color hues. The most common use is between the last row of tiles and the floor or tub. Just a thin bead of caulk will provide the same look as grout, but gives you the flexibility needed between the two surface types. Types of caulk include Silicone, Water-based Latex, Polyvinyl Acetate (PVA) and Acrylic. Each has their own benefit and drawback. Do your research to select the right kind of caulk for your project.

Very important: If caulking is loose anywhere in your home, fix it! To remove Silicone caulk use a utility knife (at a low angle) to carefully remove the caulk. For the water based types use a hair dryer (300 degrees or lower) to soften the caulk before removing. After removal, clean the area before re-applying new caulk.

Loose Tiles

Tiles usually come loose for ONE reason: something is moving! The cause could be water damage to a wall or sub-floor or insufficient support or too thin of a sub-floor. Routine caulking can help minimize loose tiles.

68

10 ELECTRICAL

A professional and licensed electrician should always perform ALL electrical work in your home.

Performing an electrical DIY or hiring a handyman who says he knows how to do electrical work is a dangerous thing to do. Electrical codes are constantly changed and upgraded for new products and techniques. Only a licensed electrician, who is required to attend classes every three years to learn the new codes, can repair and install electrical devices and systems correctly and safely.

If you have any questions, you can always check with your local municipality about the correct Permits required for any electrical job you are contemplating for your home.

Electrical Components

Your basic residential home electrical system consists of:

Electric Line (typically from a pole outside but also can be buried underground).
Meter where usage is measured (on exterior of house).
Electrical Panel (where all the switches are and usually in basement or garage).
Separate Wiring Circuits to all the rooms in the house for outlets,

Your Electrical Panel

Two things are important about your Electrical Panel.
1. Know where it is.
2. Make sure it is labeled correctly.

The Panel is divided up between the Main Circuit Breaker (usually located at the top of the Panel) and individual Circuits (located below the Main Circuit Breaker). The Main Circuit Breaker is just that. It is intended to "break" the electric current in the event of an overload. If there is an overload from outside the home, the breaker will "flip" off.

Most homes are set up with 200 amp service (older homes might only have 100 amp service and larger homes could have up to 400 amp service). Amp stands for amperage. Therefore, if your home is set up with 200 amp service, that is the total amount of electricity that your home can use at a time. Go to your Main Breaker Panel and look for the biggest breaker in the panel (usually at the top), the number on the switch identifies the total amps for your home.

Below your Main Breaker will be "circuit" breakers. The circuits are set up to feed electricity to each part of your home or to any hard wired appliance like water heaters, air conditioners, and furnaces. Circuits are not all the same size. In other words, your bedroom may only need a 15 amp circuit and your air conditioner needs a 30 amp circuit. Your kitchen, by electrical code, always requires multiple circuits. These individual "circuits" work just like the Main Circuit Breaker. If the individual circuit gets overloaded, the breaker will trip in your Electric Panel. Familiarize yourself with these breakers. Know how to flip them back on in the event of an overload.

220 vs. 110

220 volts is 2x the volume (voltage) at ½ the pace (current). The advantage of 220 is less (thinner) copper is needed to transmit energy and less energy is lost to resistance. The advantage of 110 volts is it is less likely to hurt you. Most of your house only needs 110 volts to operate. Larger appliances need 220, like your dryer, oven, water heater and furnace.

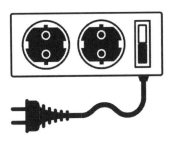

AFCIs (Arc Fault Circuit Interrupters)

An arc fault occurs when loose or corroded connections make intermittent contact which causes sparking or "arcing" between the connections. The arc creates heat which can then break down the insulation around the wire. This can cause an electrical fire. AFCIs detect "arcs" by the use of advanced electronic technology within the AFCI. This technology monitors the circuit for the presence of "normal" and "dangerous" arcing conditions. There are actually "normal" arcs in your home. Equipment such as a vacuum cleaner or furnace motor can create a normal arcing condition. However, a dangerous arc can occur for many reasons including damage of the electrical insulation. Whether it is normal or dangerous arcing, when it occurs, the AFCI analyzes the characteristics of the event and determines if it is hazardous and then reacts accordingly.

GFCIs
(Ground Fault Circuit Interrupters)

GFCI outlets are our best protection against electrical shock. This type of electrical outlet is required to be used anywhere water could be in your home (bathroom, kitchen, garage, basement, etc.). GFCIs are designed to sense when a shock is about to happen and then they shut the electricity off at the outlet. They look like typical outlets but also have a test and reset button. They should be tested monthly. Just press the test button which trips the outlet and then press the reset button to restore power. If pressing the test button or reset button doesn't work, it's time for a new GFCI outlet.

DISASTER ZONE

To save some money, Eddy and Betty thought that they would pay their son to help them turn the attic into a bonus room. Their son, Eddy Jr., did all of the wiring and it was never inspected. When Eddy & Betty went to sell the house, it cost $7,000 to bring the room up to code because all the drywall had to be torn down for the inspection. That's when they discovered the amateur electrical job, that did not pass inspection and was actually causing a fire hazard.

Using Extension Cords

Of course, permanent wiring systems have built in safety features, but extension cords do not. Know the difference between an interior extension cord and an exterior extension cord (check the label). To be safe, the extension cord wattage rating should be 1.25 times the rating of the appliance. For example, standard cords are fine for a lamp with a 100 watt bulb, but plug in a room heater and the cord can heat up and start a fire! If there is NO label on the extension cord, don't use it! Purchase the correct cord for the job.

Electrical Safety Tips

- Avoid overloading your electrical outlets. They can overheat and start a fire.
- Never use altered or fraying extension cords or surge protectors.
- Check your outlets regularly for any problems like overheating, loose connections and corrosion.
- Periodically test all your GFCIs and AFCIs to make sure they are working properly.
- Check to make sure all outdoor outlets are protected with GFCI technology to reduce the risk of shock.

A big THANK YOU to Sara Carle at Kope Electric, Lebanon, NJ for helping me provide so much great information about the electrical components in your home!

The holidays are a wonderful time for family and friends. Lighting up your house with holiday lighting decorations is fun and just adds so much to the whole experience. Here are some tips to make sure your holiday seasons stay lighted with love!

BEST TIPS FOR SAFE HOLIDAY DECORATING

- Remember to always read the manufacturer's instructions for each item to understand how to use it properly.

- Inspect electrical decorations for damage before use (frayed wires, cracks, and be sure there is a bulb in each socket). Throw away any damaged wires.

- Don't overload electrical outlets! Overloaded electrical outlets and faulty wires are a common cause of holiday fires. Don't overload! And, remember to only plug in one high-wattage appliance into each outlet at a time.

- Only purchase lights that have been approved by Underwriters Laboratory. "UL" will be clearly displayed on the tag, signifying the product has been inspected for potential safety hazards. The RED UL marks indicate the lights are safe for **indoor/outdoor** use, and the GREEN UL marks indicate the lights are only safe for **indoor** use.

- Never connect more than three strings of incandescent lights. More than three can blow a fuse and start a fire.

- Protect cords from damage. Cords should never be pinched by furniture, forced into small spaces like doors or windows, placed under rugs, located near heat sources or attached by nails or staples.

- Prevent tripping by placing cords and decorations in low-traffic areas where they won't be walked on. Avoid twisting, kinking or crushing cords.

- For outdoor decorating, keep ladders and decorations away from overhead power lines. Make sure the ladder is securely placed on the ground before climbing.

- Don't use tacks or nails to connect outdoor electrical cords and lights, instead use clips to safely attach lights to the house.

- For outdoors, only use heavy-duty extension cords specifically designed for outdoor use. Avoid overloading extension cords by using no more than three sets of standard lights per cord.

- If possible, outdoor lights and inflatable decorations should be plugged into circuits protected by ground fault circuit interrupters (GFCI). GFCIs help prevent electric shock by breaking the circuits when needed.

- Turn off and unplug all holiday decorations before going to sleep or leaving the house.

- Additionally, if you have children in your home, use safety caps on all electrical outlets that are not in use to prevent shock. Keep sharp objects out of reach, as well as items that could be swallowed.

Generators

There are two types of generators: portable and stand by. Both types come in various sizes (kilowatts) to supply the electricity you need in an outage.

A portable generator is more budget friendly but requires your manual efforts as a homeowner for operation. They are generally fueled with gasoline and you will need a manual transfer switch or interlock switch kit installed by a licensed electrician for a portable generator to work safely. With portable generators you also must be very careful about their exhaust (they should ALWAYS be outside and not in a garage).

An automatic standby generator powers your home off of your natural gas utility or propane tanks. An automatic transfer switch (ATS) is installed next to your main electrical panel by a licensed electrician. This switch reacts when power is lost and turns on the generator (and likewise when power is restored it turns off the generator). You need both a licensed electrician (who installs the transfer switch) and a licensed plumber (who properly sizes the generator and inbound gas pressure).

For either generator project, check with your local code enforcement before signing any contract. Permits are required for your safety to be sure all calculations are accurate, manufacturer install specifications are followed, and exhaust clearances are met. Local ordinances and homeowner's associations may also have noise and aesthetic regulations to consider as well.

Both types of back up power solutions also require seasonal maintenance. Just like your car or lawn mower, generators, both portable and standby, require oil changes, filter changes, and seasonal TLC.

Do generators have to be maintained?

Yes, simple maintenance is required. All generators require periodic oil and filter changes to ensure maximum performance for years of reliable service.

Portable Generators Can Be Dangerous

Portable generators should be used with extreme caution.

- Always make sure the portable generator is outside because they expel carbon monoxide (never have one in the garage).

- Make sure your electric panel is wired correctly. If you are going to use a portable generator, first have your electrician check your panel.

- You must maintain the fuel level in a portable generator. Any loss of power due to no fuel wreaks havoc on circuit boards commonly found on HVAC, garage door and most electronics.

- Be very careful how you store your gas/fuel for a portable generator.

Why should I buy an automatic standby generator instead of a portable generator?

During a utility power outage, an automatic standby generator provides numerous advantages over a portable generator:

- The American Red Cross recommends permanently installed standby generators as a safer way to provide backup power to a home than a portable generator.
- With an automatic standby generator properly installed outside, your home is protected from deadly carbon monoxide poisoning that is a much greater risk with portable generators. Automatic generators actually do emit carbon dioxide, it's just that they are always installed outside and away from windows and vents.
- Running on the home's natural gas or LP fuel supply, it is less expensive to run than gasoline and does not need to be refilled.
- They start automatically within seconds of a power outage, and eliminate the need to haul a portable generator outside or run extension cords throughout your home.
- They provide protection 24/7, whether you're home or away, and they turn themselves off when utility power returns, so there is no need to monitor the unit during an outage.

74

11 CHIMNEYS & EXHAUST PIPES

People typically think of chimneys as being the old brick or stone things that Santa Claus climbs down. However, chimneys are now made of many different materials and are for different uses in your home. They may even simply be cosmetic (typically referred to as a chimney chase). Instead of a chimney, many homes may have flue pipes or exhaust vent pipes for venting the combustion gases from their water heater or heating unit (boiler, furnace, etc.).

EXHAUST PIPES

Any appliance (boiler, water heater, furnace, etc.) that relies on combustion for heat will have some form of exhaust pipe. This can be either a PVC direct vent pipe or a metal vent pipe. These can exhaust either through the wall or roof. These are typically inspected and certified whenever an appliance is replaced and/or maintained (they should be inspected during your annual heating and air conditioning tune ups).

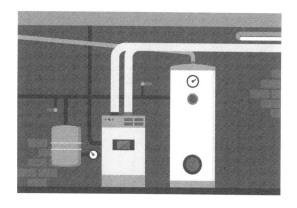

MASONRY CHIMNEYS

There are over 25,000 chimney fires per year in the United States. Therefore, any traditional chimneys should be inspected by a professional chimney contractor to ensure that they are in sound condition and safe for use. If the mortar joints have failed, and/or the masonry liners are cracked or separated, a fire inside the chimney could escape and get into the framing of your house. If the inside of your masonry chimney has been compromised, but the exterior of the chimney is sound, a stainless steel liner can be installed to protect this from occurring.

Chimneys, liners and flues for wood burning stoves or fireplaces should be cleaned yearly, if not more, depending on their usage.

SEPTIC SYSTEMS

According to the EPA, one-fourth of U.S. homes use a septic system. All of those homes together put more than 4 billion gallons of wastewater per day below the ground's surface. If your septic system isn't working properly, you just might be contaminating your own ground water and the ground water of your neighbors.

The EPA recommends that septic systems be inspected at least every 3 years by a professional septic company. They also suggest that you have your tank pumped regularly (generally every 3 to 4 years). When you schedule your septic professional to come out, make sure they do the following. The most important thing is for the professional to show you where the plumbing lines, access holes and tank are located. Put them on a drawing of your property and keep records so you can note any changes over the years.

What your professional inspection should include:

- Locating the system.

- Uncovering access holes.

- Flushing the toilets.

- Checking for signs of back up.

- Measuring scum and sludge layers.

- Identifying any leaks.

- Inspecting mechanical components.

- Pumping the tank, if necessary.

DISASTER ZONE

Jesse was a city girl who moved to the country for her job. She rented a house with a septic system and didn't even realize it. When she had a back up of waste into her shower, she was shocked! The landlord said the septic tank had been pumped recently and couldn't understand what happened. The landlord called a professional who figured out that the leach field was clogged causing the back up. Jesse wanted to move back to the city!

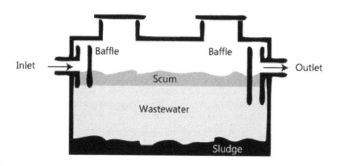

What can I do to protect my septic system?

Know where everything is (plumbing lines, tank, access holes & the drainfield). Periodically inspect those four areas for leaking.

Change your toilets out to 1.6 gallon. Many homes still have 3.5 to 5 gallon reservoirs. You can save thousands of gallons of water with a high-efficiency toilet. Also, make sure your toilets are not leaking -- leaky toilets can waste as much as 200 gallons of water a day.

Use faucet aerators and high-efficiency showerheads – both of which help reduce water use. If you see a faucet leak, take care of it right away.

Be mindful of how much water you are putting into your septic system every day (turn off faucets while shaving or brushing your teeth; run dishwasher and washing machine when full only). The less work your septic system has to do the longer it will last.

DON'T FLUSH these things down your toilet:

- dental floss
- feminine hygiene products
- condoms
- diapers
- cotton swabs
- cigarette butts
- coffee grounds
- cat litter
- paper towels
- household chemicals
- cleaning agents
- gasoline
- oil
- pesticides
- antifreeze
- paint

DON'T do all your household laundry in one day. Doing load after load can be harmful to your septic system because the tank doesn't have time to adequately treat the waste and you could be flooding your drainfield without allowing sufficient recovery time. The best thing to do is spread your laundry out over the week.

- DO invest in a new clothes washing machine. The new Energy Star washer uses 35% less energy and 50% less water than the standard model.
- Plant only grass on your drainfield. NEVER plant trees or bushes.
- Don't ever drive or park on your drainfield. The vehicle weight can compact the soil and possibly damage the pipes.
- Keep roof gutters/leaders and basement sump pump drains away from the drainfield. Flooding the drainfield can slow down or even stop the treatment process which in turn can cause your plumbing fixtures to back up.

13 LANDSCAPING & IRRIGATION TIPS

When it comes to landscaping your property, anything goes.

Think about your style. Landscaping is very much like decorating the inside of your home. You want it to reflect you. For example, I don't like very stylized, organized and rigid shrubs and trees. I like flowy grasses and flowering trees, groundcovers and interesting shrubs. Others love the very stylized look. Drive around and look at what others are doing to help determine what you like the best. Also, think about what fits the architectural design of the home. You might love cactus, but putting a cactus in front of your Victorian home just might be weird. Also, look at the fences, pavers, front walks, and raised tree beds for ideas.

Just like in real estate, location matters. Get out your sketch book and start drawing ideas.

▷ What areas will be installed or replaced? Trees, shrubs/beds, walkways, patios, grill area, spa area, pool, fencing, raised garden area.

▷ Where are the water sources?

▷ Do you need a gas line to a grill or fireplace?

▷ Will there be a storage shed?

▷ What about landscape lighting? Irrigation?

Try and think through the entire project and process. It might take several sketches before you get it all down. Take photos of areas you like and keep a file of landscapes you love from magazines, etc. Also, ask family and friends for their ideas too.

Other basic considerations

- Your geographic area's seasons, soil type and wild game issues (some areas have large deer herds that eat residential landscaping plants). All will have an impact on your landscaping.
- Will you consider alternatives to grass?
- What is the drainage like on your property?
- Always keep in mind that shrubs and trees should be planted away from the sides of your home. You always want air flow in and around your home.
- Also, make sure all gutters and leaders stay clear and are directed away from the home.
- What is your water source? Well or city.
- Where is your septic system?
- Will you install an irrigation system? If so, do you need to treat the water first?
- Will you be installing fencing around the perimeter of your property?
- Know where all underground lines and pipes are. Always call before your dig!

Shop Local

Shop local and get to know your local nursery and landscape professionals. They can help you too. Even if you are a do-it-yourselfer, if you are completely overhauling your landscape, a consultation and plan from a landscape architect will help tremendously.

Next, develop a budget. Here are some budget considerations. Remember to count time and materials. Give yourself an hourly rate and track the time you spend on your project. That way, you will know what it really costs you.

Costs

- Include demo time and if you need a dumpster or trailer to remove everything from the property. Also, will remaining stumps need to be ground up? Figure in the cost of that too.
- What tools or equipment do you need to borrow or purchase?
- Cost to do it yourself vs. hiring a professional?
- Do some of it yourself and have a professional do some?
- Cost of new shrubs. Materials plus labor to install.
- Cost of annuals and installation. What about bulbs?
- Installing an irrigation system? Consider all costs associated. You might also need a building permit to install an irrigation system.
- Installing landscape lighting? What is the plan and costs associated?
- Pavers, fences, decks, water features, fire pits and fire places. Costs for installing a gas line for a grill or fireplace?
- Consider alternatives to traditional grass (ground covers, Fescue and ornamental grasses, flowers, herbs, vegetables, native plants, moss, mulch, lavender, perennials, succulents and ferns, pollinator habitats like meadows and flower beds, hardscapes and paths, artificial turf).
- Also develop an ongoing maintenance budget for your exterior property so that you will be ready to repair or replace something in the future.

Do-It-Yourselfers

For the do-it-yourselfers, try and do all the demo that is required throughout the property at the same time. You might need a dumpster or trailer to remove all the old shrubs/trees, etc. and it's just easier and cheaper to do the demo all at once. Then, organize your plan into areas to be tackled. It is always better to pick an area that you know you can start and finish. Then, move on down the plan.

LANDSCAPE IRRIGATION

The most efficient and ecological way to get water to your landscape (lawn, shrub beds, trees) is through a landscape irrigation system. These systems include both irrigation heads that pop up to water a designated area as well as in-ground "drip" systems that consist of tubing under the ground (usually under the mulch) and usually for shrub and tree beds. Many systems can be managed via apps on your phone too.

In colder climates, irrigation systems must be closed for the winter and opened for the summer. This is typically done with an air compressor. In some areas there are self-draining features that can be utilized to drain a system during cold weather. Either way, make sure and get it done before the first freeze! And, know how to shut the water off to the irrigation system. (Label it different from your main water supply.)

Most irrigation companies offer service contracts for the opening, closing and ongoing maintenance of an irrigation system.

Irrigation professionals should be licensed and insured. There are also many certifications that irrigation professionals can earn. Like all the trades, technology has really helped irrigation systems get even more efficient through analyzing water needs to determine when and how much an area should be watered. Irrigation professionals might also work with backyard ponds, waterfalls, green roofs, wildlife drinkers, equestrian arenas and landscape lighting.

If you are on a city water system, know how to read your water meter. And, understand if it has an indicator to show if there is a leak or not. Consider reading the indicator more frequently than the water company does. Because if they read it quarterly, it could be 3 months before you even know you have a problem.

If you are on a well system, discuss with your well driller professional whether your well has the capacity to fully supply an irrigation system during the peak dry periods without running the well dry. Also, discuss with your irrigation specialist whether you are short cycling your well pump (which means it shuts off and turns on frequently). Short cycling can damage a well pump. Lastly, if your well water requires conditioning for your domestic use, the question to ask is if the irrigation system requires conditioned water.

If at all possible, use drip irrigation to help conserve water.

Washing Machines

If your washing machine hose bursts, it's a BIG deal! Why? Because the water will run constantly. That means water will flow out at about 650 gallons per hour flooding everything. Here are a few things you can do to prevent that from ever happening in your home.

- Turn off the washing machine valve after every use.
- Never leave a washing machine going if you are not home.
- Check the condition of the hoses to make sure there are no kinks.
- Install washing machine hoses with at least a 5-year warranty.
- Check your washing machine drain hoses too. Look for discoloration or rust and replace them immediately if you see any leaks.

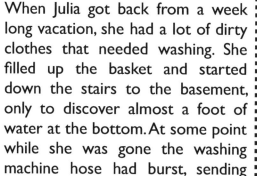

DISASTER ZONE

When Julia got back from a week long vacation, she had a lot of dirty clothes that needed washing. She filled up the basket and started down the stairs to the basement, only to discover almost a foot of water at the bottom. At some point while she was gone the washing machine hose had burst, sending thousands of gallons of water straight into the basement. She had no idea it was possible to turn the pipe off between uses.

How to clean your washing machine.

Did you know that washing machines can become a breeding ground for salmonella and other germs? When you clean certain whites in hot water, your washing machine is being cleaned as well. But, once a month, run an empty load with hot water and white vinegar to sanitize the basin and wipe out any lingering germs.

Dryers & Dryer Vent Cleaning

There are more than 15,000 dryer vent fires every year in the United States. Dryer vent fires are a real problem in newer, bigger homes where the dryer is placed in the center of the house and not up against an outside wall. Some of these dryer vents can run 15, 20, 25 feet to exhaust to the outside – that's a lot of length and twists and turns. Also, older dryer vent piping can become brittle, causing lint to build up which in turn causes a potential fire hazard.

Here are some of the signs that it's time to clean your vent:
- Clothes are not completely dry after 35 to 40 minutes.
- You smell a musty odor in the clothing after drying.
- Clothing seems unusually hot after a complete drying cycle.
- The dryer vent hood flap does not properly open.
- Debris is noticed within the outside dryer vent opening.
- Excessive heat is noticed in the laundry room.
- Large amounts of lint accumulate in the lint trap.
- A visible sign of lint is noticed around the lint filter for the dryer.

Using "dryer sheets" to add fragrance or to reduce static cling can cause a film to clog the mesh of the lint filter. Usually, you can't even see it, but the clog can block the flow of air slowing the dryer process and causing excessive heat build up. Use a toothbrush and warm, soapy water to clean the filter every six months.

Refrigerators

Have you checked the door seal on your refrigerator lately? You want the seal to be tight which reduces the amount of energy needed to keep food at the right temperature. To test, close the door on a piece of paper. If the paper slides out with hardly any resistance, it might be time to replace the door seals. Periodically vacuum the coils behind the refrigerator. Cleaning these coils regularly helps the refrigerator to run more efficiently, extending the life of the unit.

Most importantly, check those ice maker hoses! If they leak or burst, water keeps running! The hoses should be copper or stainless steel. However, it is not unusual to find a plastic hose. If you have a plastic ice maker water hose, consider changing it to copper or stainless steel.

Garbage Disposals

Whatever you do to clean a garbage disposal, just remember to NEVER put boiling water down your kitchen sink/garbage disposal. Boiling water can damage plastic pipes. There are several different ways to clean garbage disposals. Here are a few.

- The easiest way to clean a garbage disposal is to fill up the sink with 2-4" of hot water with a little dishwasher soap in it. Pull the plug and run the garbage disposal which will push all that hot soapy water through it.
- Or you can fill the drain with two cups of ice, pour one cup of rock salt over the ice, run the cold water and turn on the disposal until it is all gone. This will help clean the grime and debris from the grinding elements in the garbage disposal.
- You can also add half a lemon or lime, run the cold water while the disposal grinds up the fruit – this helps to clean and deodorize your drain.

Dishwashers

Dishwashers really NEED to be cleaned every so often. Gunk from grease, soap scum and leftover food can wreak havoc to a dishwasher over time.

- Clean the filter. The filter's job is to collect the gunk so you can imagine it's pretty dirty. The filter is usually located at the bottom, unscrew it and soak it in warm soapy water for about 15 minutes. Use a toothbrush to gently scrub the filter.
- Clean the inside of the dishwasher. Again, use a toothbrush dipped in soapy water or a baking soda paste to gently clean away any gunk around the door seal, spray arm, or any other areas.
- Deodorize with vinegar. Just pour a cup of white vinegar into the bottom of your empty dishwasher and run a heavy cycle.

Stoves, Ovens

- Ovens should be properly sealed. Check the rubber gasket along the edge of the door to make sure it's not cracking, warping or has become loose. Replace if you see any of those conditions.
- Ovens should be cleaned twice a year, maybe more if you cook a lot. Either use your self-clean function or do it the old fashioned way with water, baking soda and vinegar.
- NEVER clean under the knobs with water or cleaning mixtures. Why? Because there is an electrical system under the knob – so, if you remove the knobs and spray liquid cleaner, you are essentially dousing an electrical system. Instead, spray your paper towel or cleaning rag and then carefully wipe away the grease and grime.

15 GENERAL CLEANING TIPS

If you follow these tips and create a system for yourself, your house cleaning will be efficient and effective.

- Use natural cleaning products, if possible. Vinegar, ammonia, baking soda, lemon juice, toothpaste and water are some of the most common natural cleaning products. Just remember to NEVER combine ammonia-based cleaners with chlorine bleach or products containing bleach (such as powdered dishwasher detergent). The combination will create dangerous fumes. ALWAYS read the product labels or do your research before you mix anything for cleaning.
- Keep your cleaning supplies in one place.
- When it is time to clean, use a bucket or basket to carry all your cleaning supplies.
- Clean one room at a time. Always try to de-clutter a room first.
- Always start at the top and work your way down.
- Work from the back of the room to the front of the room and from left to right.
- Dust first (from top to bottom), then vacuum. Use a slightly damp rag to dust to stop the dust from becoming airborne.
- Use separate rubber gloves for kitchen and bathroom work (for obvious reasons).
- Vacuum yourself out of the room - no footprints!
- Make a schedule, get the whole family involved and stick to it!

DISASTER ZONE

Fred and Mae had just finished repainting the kitchen when Fred decided to sand and refinish the wood beams. Fred just didn't think about the dust. Well, there was so much dust everywhere on the newly painted surfaces that months later Mae is still noticing the light brown dust on the walls and ceilings. And, Mae is not happy about it.

CAUTION CAUTION

ORGANIZE YOUR GARAGE

Set aside the time (probably a whole day or weekend!).
Find a family member or friend to help out (offer a bribe!).
Make a list of what you want to **KEEP** in your garage.

Garbage/Recycle area

Tools

Toys

Sports/hunting equipment

Cleaning supplies

General storage area

Automotive supplies

Luggage

Camping gear

Seasonal décor

Food storage area

Toilet paper/paper towel storage area

Lawn/Leaf tools

Pet supplies & food

Before you invest in storage bins or systems, collect a bunch of cardboard boxes, tarps or use chalk marks on the garage floor to designate a "group". Use the boxes, tarps or designated areas to group the items you will be keeping, donating or tossing.

To begin the process, put all "like" things together in their categories and determine what stays, what is donated and what is trash. Go through each of the above categories one at a time and remove the <u>trash</u> and donation piles from the garage before you start the next category.

Wait until you have gone through the <u>entire garage </u>before you determine your storage system. Be creative. There are a lot of furniture type items that can be re-purposed for organizing "things". The goal is to purchase only what you need.

Ways to Organize Creatively, Safely & On a Budget

- Determine best layout for everything that is staying.
- The goal is to keep as much "stuff" off the floor as possible (much easier to clean floor if most everything is off the floor).
- Paint the walls a fun color.
- Paint the concrete floor with an antiskid product.
- Install a fire extinguisher & carbon monoxide detector.

- Pegboards and hooks (for tools with outlines of tool drawn on them).
- Slat wall or pallets can be used to hang small tools and sports equipment.
- Use cloth shoe holders for small tools, cleaning supplies or sports equipment.
- Hang bikes vertically or from the ceiling.
- Or mark off an area with colored tape for kids to park their bikes.
- Use an old chest of drawers for storage. Secure to wall.
- Keep a fold-up worktable handy.
- Keep a small foldable ladder handy.
- Use a magnetic strip for small metal tools.
- Use large plastic garbage cans for rakes, shoves, brooms, patio umbrellas, etc.
- Spackle buckets can be used for a lot of small items.
- Use an old book case for your boot/shoe rack. Secure to wall.
- Store and dispose of any paint correctly.
- If you do purchase bins, make sure they have CLEAR lids.
- If you use boxes, mark them clearly with their contents.
- Think about purchasing a lockable storage cabinet for lawn chemicals, insecticides and other items you don't want children or pets getting near.
- Make sure the bottom of your garage door sits flush with the floor (to keep out leaves, bugs, mice). If it doesn't, install a rubberized strip made for garage doors.
- Make sure the auto-reverse on your garage door opener is working correctly. Check frequently.

16 ENERGY SAVING TIPS

Home heating and cooling account for almost half of a home's energy use, while water heating accounts for 18%, making these some of the largest energy expenses in any home. A home energy audit can help you:

- Understand the whole picture of your home's energy use.
- Determine how much energy your home uses.
- Determine where energy is being lost.
- Determine the priority of what to fix first to make your home more efficient and comfortable.

Of course, a professional home energy audit is the best way to determine where you might be losing energy. But, you can actually conduct your own home energy audit by following these tips from the U.S. Department of Energy. The Department also recommends to NOT assume that just because your home is recently constructed–or even new–that there are no opportunities to save energy. It is important to note that energy-saving technology has evolved rapidly over the past few years, outpacing training commonly available to many builders. And, certainly, before any remodel job or before the installation of any new heating equipment, a home energy audit should be performed.

How to Conduct Your Own Energy Audit

- Keep a checklist: when walking through your home, keep a checklist of areas you have inspected and problems you found. This list will help you prioritize your energy efficiency upgrades.
- Inside the house locate air leaks/drafts along the baseboard or edge of the flooring and at junctures of the walls and ceiling.
- Outside the house check for leaks, especially in areas where two different building materials meet.
- Other places to check for leaks include windows, doors, lighting and plumbing fixtures, switches, and electrical outlets. Also check for open fireplace dampers.
- Check insulation. Heat loss from inadequate or missing insulation can be very large.
- Inspect heating and cooling equipment. This equipment should be inspected and tuned up by a professional annually or as recommended by the manufacturer. And, don't forget to change that air filter!
- Check your lighting. Energy for lighting accounts for about 10% of your electric bill. Replace all bulbs with energy-saving incandescents, compact fluorescent lamps (CFLs), or light-emitting diodes (LEDs). When shopping for bulbs, consider the brightness of the bulbs and look for ways to use controls such as sensors, dimmers, or timers to reduce lighting use.

General Tips to Save Energy

- Take shorter showers to reduce water heating costs.

- Don't waste money on electronics or appliances that aren't in use. Turn off and unplug unused televisions and DVD players, computers, phone chargers, coffee makers and other devices.

- Keep your refrigerator coils clean and don't set the temperature too low, making the unit work too hard.

- Wash full loads of laundry using cold water. Modern detergents work great in cold water, and about 90 percent of the energy used by clothes washers goes to water heating.

- Clean the lint trap in the clothes dryer before every cycle.

- Turn off water when not needed while brushing teeth, shaving or doing dishes.

- Use the self-cleaning oven feature only when necessary. Start the self-cleaning cycle immediately after you use the oven in order to take advantage of pre-existing heat.

- Open the oven door infrequently. Every time you open it, the temperature drops about 25 F to 30 F, and more energy is used to generate the desired level of heat.

- Operate your dishwasher with full loads, and air-dry dishes on the energy saver setting. If the manufacturer's instructions permit, open the dishwasher door at the end of the last rinse cycle, rather than using the drying cycle.

- Install energy-saving showerheads, faucets or flow restrictors.

- Use dimmer switches or timers on your lights.

- Replace incandescent bulbs with compact fluorescent lamps that give the same amount and quality of light as incandescent bulbs, yet use one-quarter the amount of energy and last 10 times longer.

- Select an energy-efficient model ENERGY STAR® labeled refrigerator, washer, air conditioner or other appliance.

- When shopping for a printer, scanner or other computer peripherals, spend a few extra dollars to buy one that automatically goes into sleep mode or turns off when not in use.

- Replace your old windows with high-efficiency ENERGY STAR® windows. Doing so could reduce your heating and cooling costs by up to 15 percent.

- Install a door sweep on your garage door to seal the gap between the bottom of the door and the threshold. The door sweep prevents cold air from coming in and warm air from escaping your home.

- Insulate the spaces between your walls with foam. Homes often leak warm air in the winter because of spaces between walls. Fill these gaps by spraying foam insulation into holes drilled in the wall.

Tips to Save Energy on Warm Days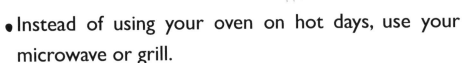

- Instead of using your oven on hot days, use your microwave or grill.
- Keep debris away from your outside air conditioner.
- Set your thermostat between 75F and 78F on warm days. Set it to 85 F when you're away for more than a few hours.
- Don't do your laundry and cooking until cooler times of the day.
- Use your ceiling fan when using your air conditioner. It can actually raise your thermostat about four degrees Fahrenheit to save on cooling costs with no reduction in comfort.
- Make sure the fresh air vent on your air conditioner is closed so you are not spending extra money on cooling the outside air.
- For your bathroom and kitchen ventilation fans, turn them off about 10 minutes after their job is done to keep them from pushing cooled air out of your house.
- Hang laundry outside. Give your dryer a break and save some money!
- Teach everyone in your home to turn off the lights in rooms that aren't in use.
- Windows: open them in the morning and at night for cooler air flow into your home. Cover your windows during the day to block the hot sun.
- Check the filter on your air conditioning system, and clean or replace it if it's dirty. A dirty filter slows air flow and causes your system to use more energy.
- Outdoor awnings over windows and doors can protect your home from the hot sun year-round.
- You can also paint your house a light color to reflect heat.

Tips to Save Energy on Cold Days

- If you are using your fireplace, turn down your furnace/heater. When you're not using your fireplace, make sure to close the damper to keep out cold air.

- Keep your curtains, shades and blinds closed at night and even during the day, if you are not home. They help prevent warm air from escaping.

- Set your furnace thermostat to **68** degrees Fahrenheit (**68 F**) or lower, health permitting. Three to five percent more energy is used for each degree you set your furnace above **68 F**.

- When you leave the house, set your thermostat to 56 F. If you turn your thermostat back 10 to 15 degrees for eight hours, you can actually save five to 15 percent a year on your heating bill.

- Make annual inspections to make sure windows, doors, gaps and cracks are caulked to prevent cold air from entering your home.

- Wrap older water heaters with an insulating jacket or blanket to minimize excess heat loss. Remember to leave the air intake vent uncovered.

- Make sure your attic is properly insulated. Doing so may result in a savings of up to 10 percent of your total energy costs.

17 WATER SAVING TIPS

ONLY YOU CAN SAVE WATER!

Why save water? Let me count the ways:

- Money: Save money on your water bill by monitoring it for unusually high use. To check the water meter, read the meter before and after a two-hour period when no water is being used.   If the meter changes, there is a leak.

- Prevent Pollution: Help prevent and reduce water pollution in nearby lakes, rivers and local watersheds.

- Extend the life of your septic system.

- Save municipal sewer systems: Reduced water means reduction in the possible overloading of water systems (which can result in untreated sewage flowing into nearby lakes and rivers).

- Save electricity: Power plants use thousands of gallons of water to cool. Saving energy saves water!

The World Health Organization says it takes about 7 gallons of water per day to cover basic hygiene, food production and food hygiene for the average world wide citizen.

It is amazing how what you eat increases the use of water. If you eat less meat and dairy, you will be using less water. According to National Geographic, it takes approximately 1,000 gallons per person per day to produce the average American diet -- that is 100 gallons more per day than the global average water footprint of 900 gallons for diet, household use, transportation, energy and the consumption of material goods. Also, choose grass-fed rather than grain-fed, since it can take a lot of water to grow corn and other feed crops.   On average a vegan, who doesn't eat meat or dairy, indirectly consumes 600 gallons of water per day less than a person who eats the average American diet.

While we can't do everything, certainly we can do something. Thanks to all the state environmental agencies across the country who posted all these great tips on their different websites, especially the western states, where water conservation is front and center in their lives.

Together we can all save water. Go through this list room by room with your family and identify the things that you can do to save water. You will be glad you did.

Americans use about 100 gallons of water per day!

Europeans use about 50 gallons of water per day!

Sub-Saharan Africans use about 5 gallons per day!

KITCHEN

There are many ways to save water in the kitchen. Turn these into habits!

- When washing dishes by hand, don't let the water run. Fill one basin with wash water and the other with rinse water. If you have a single-basin sink, put dishes on a rack or in a pan full of hot water to rinse.
- Dishwashers typically use less water than washing dishes by hand. New ENERGY STAR® dishwashers save even more water and energy.
- Learn how to load your dishwasher in the most efficient manner. It matters where you place your plates, glasses, pots and pans, plastic and cutlery.
- If you have a new dishwasher, it is possible to cut back on rinsing because newer models clean more thoroughly than older ones.
- Soak pots and pans instead of letting the water run while you scrape them clean.
- Use water bottles for your daily intake of water. This cuts down on glasses to wash.
- Garbage disposals use a lot of water to process the food. Use them sparingly. Compost your food waste and save gallons of water.
- Use a pan of water to wash your fruits and vegetables instead of running water from the tap.
- Always defrost food in the refrigerator. Don't use running water to thaw food.
- Keep a pitcher of drinking water in the refrigerator instead of running the tap. This way, every drop goes down you and not the drain.
- Plan your meals and try to reuse leftover water from cooked or steamed foods to make soup.
- Cook food in as little water as possible. This also helps it retain more nutrients.
- Select the proper pan size for cooking. Large pans may require more cooking water than necessary.
- If you accidentally drop ice cubes, don't throw them in the sink. Drop them in a house plant instead.
- Collect the water you use while rinsing fruit and vegetables. Use it to water house plants.
- Look into installing an instant water heater near your kitchen sink. The closer the water heater, the less time it takes to heat up. Less water and less energy!

LAUNDRY ROOM

Your laundry room uses a lot of water! Here are some tips to reduce that usage amount.

• Learn to say no to hot water. Today's washing machines and detergents have been designed to work in cold water. When you want to brighten whites, use cold water and a bleach alternative. If a family member is sick, use hot water mixed with chlorine bleach to reduce bacteria in the bed linens and towels. The same goes for cleaning dirty cloth diapers.

• When buying a washer, consider buying a front-loading machine. Front-loading machines are energy and water efficient using just over 20 gallons a load, while most top-loading machines use 40 gallons per load. And, of course, look for the ENERGY STAR® rating of any new machine.

• When doing laundry, match the water level to the size of the load.

• Did you know the permanent press cycle uses an extra five gallons per wash? If you don't really need it, don't use it!

• Consider having a plumber re-route your grey water to trees and plants rather than the sewer line. Always check local codes before doing any plumbing work.

DISASTER ZONE

Paula was a very busy single parent with three daughters! The only time she had to do the laundry was on the weekend. So every Sunday afternoon she knew she would be doing load after load. What she didn't realize was that she was overloading her septic field with water and soap. And once a system becomes overloaded with fluid, solid waste moves into the leach field and can quickly block the entire process causing a backup. Paula learned the hard way when her septic backed up into the house. What's the lesson here? Spread your laundry out throughout the week if you are on a septic system. It will certainly help to keep your system working correctly.

BATHROOM
There are many ways to save water in the bathroom.

• New toilets use so much less water! Therefore, if your toilet was installed before 1992, you should really think about purchasing a WaterSense® labeled toilet. You will save water with every flush!

• If possible, install a dual-flush toilet -- it has two flush options: a half-flush for liquid waste and a full-flush for solid waste.

• Toilet leaks are not always obvious! Be sure to test your toilet for leaks at least once a year. Put food coloring in your toilet tank, wait an hour and see if the water turns color.

• If your toilet flapper doesn't close properly after flushing, replace it.

• In some parts of the U.S. (particularly the west), they have a motto…"If it's yellow, let it mellow." Toilet flushing is one of the most water-intensive features in your house. Do you have to flush every time?

• Just a minute or two shorter shower will save up to 150 gallons per month. But, if you time your shower to keep it under 5 minutes, you can save up to 1,000 gallons per month!

• If you turn off the shower water while you are washing your hair, you can save up to 150 gallons a month.

- When washing your hands, turn the water off while you lather with soap.
- Plug the bathtub before turning on the water. Adjust the temperature as the tub fills. If you can, avoid baths because a full bathtub requires 70 gallons of water.

- Use a WaterSense® labeled showerhead. They're inexpensive, easy to install, and can save you up to 750 gallons a month.
- Check your faucets and showerheads for leaks. One drip every second adds up to five gallons per day!
- A family of four can save 200 gallons a week if everyone turns off the water while they are brushing their teeth!
- When shaving, instead of running the water to clean the razor, plug the sink. This simple action can save up to 300 gallons a month.
- Install water-saving aerators on all of your faucets. Not only do aerators save water, they are cheap to install.
- Don't use the toilet as a garbage can (put tissues in the trash instead of flushing them and save water every time).
- Look for WaterSense® labeled toilets, sink faucets, urinals and showerheads.
- While you wait for hot water, collect the running water and use it to water plants.
- At home or while staying in a hotel, reuse your towels.

OUTDOOR TIPS
To Save Water

GENERAL OUTDOOR
Nearly 60% of a person's household water footprint can go toward lawn and garden maintenance. Here are some general lawn tips to lower that percentage for you.

- Before the first freeze, make sure and winterize your outdoor water spigots to prevent pipes from leaking or bursting.
- Insulate all water pipes for more immediate hot water and energy savings. This is easy to do with pre-slit foam insulation.
- Wash your car on the lawn. If you do use a commercial car wash, make sure they have recycled water. If washing your car at home, use a nozzle or turn off the water (you will save at least 100 gallons every time).
- Give your pets their baths in outdoor lawn areas that need water.
- When cleaning out fish tanks, give the nutrient-rich water to your non-edible plants.
- Use a broom instead of a hose to clean patios, sidewalks and driveways, and save water every time.

- Set water softeners for a minimum number of refills to save both water and chemicals, plus energy, too.
- Report broken pipes, leaky hydrants and errant sprinklers to property owners or your local water provider.
- Know where your master water shut-off valve is located and teach everyone in the home how to turn the water off. This could save you hundreds if not thousands of gallons of water and prevent damage.
- When the kids want to cool off, use the sprinkler in an area where your lawn needs it most.
- Reward kids for the water-saving tips they follow.
- Avoid recreational water toys that require a constant flow of water.

LAWN CARE

- Hire a qualified professional to install your irrigation system and keep it working properly and efficiently.
- Adjust your lawn mower to the height of 1.5 to 2 inches. Taller grass shades roots and holds soil moisture better than short grass.
- Leave lawn clippings on your grass, this cools the ground and holds in moisture.
- If installing a lawn, select a lawn mix or blend that matches your climate and site conditions.
- Aerate your lawn periodically. Holes every six inches will allow water to reach the roots, rather than run off the surface.
- If walking across the lawn leaves footprints (blades don't spring back up), then it is time to water.
- Let your lawn go dormant (brown) during the winter. Dormant grass only needs to be watered every three to four weeks, less if it rains.
- Avoid overseeding your lawn with winter grass. Ryegrass needs water every few days, whereas Dormant Bermuda grass needs water monthly.
- Weed your lawn and garden regularly. Weeds compete with other plants for nutrients, light and water.
- While fertilizers promote plant growth, they also increase water consumption. Apply the minimum amount of fertilizer needed.
- Water your summer lawns once every three days and your winter lawn once every five days.
- Water early in the morning in the cooler temperatures which means losing less water to evaporation. Watering in the evenings can promote mold growth.
- Better yet, lose the lawn completely. Try xeriscaping your property and incorporate water wise ground cover, succulents and other plants that can thrive in drought or low water conditions.

POOL
The average pool takes 22,000 gallons of water to fill.

- Use a pool cover to help keep your pool clean, reduce chemical use and prevent water loss through evaporation.
- Make sure your swimming pools, fountains and ponds are equipped with re-circulating pumps.
- If you have an automatic refilling device, check your pool periodically for leaks.
- When back-washing your pool, consider using the water on salt-tolerant plants in the landscape.
- Minimize or eliminate the use of waterfalls and sprays in your pool. Aeration increases evaporation.
- Don't overfill the pool. Lower water levels will reduce water loss due to splashing.
- Keep water in the pool when playing, it will save water.
- Instead of building a private pool, join a community pool.
- Trickling or cascading fountains lose less water to evaporation than those that spray water into the air.
- Avoid recreational water toys that require a constant flow of water.

18 SMART HOMES

For many of us, technology has become our best friend. A friend that is there to help and support us. It is quite amazing to see technology that actively interacts with us, suggesting movies and restaurants and then booking the car service to pick us up. Knowing when we arrive home to open the garage door, turn the lights on and turn on our favorite music before we even enter our home. Explaining the answer to any question. All we have to do is ask our digital assistant and he/she makes it happen.

If you have a chance to tour a new-build "smart home", do it! The builder pre-installs all of the hard wiring for wireless access points, wi-fi capabilities for streaming, outlets, switches, sound and video delivery for the entire home and it's exterior too. Everything is connected and can be controlled through an app on your smart phone or through voice control.

What can you control and do in a smart home?

LIGHTS - INSIDE & OUTSIDE

Smart lighting systems can detect when someone is in the room and adjusts the lighting as needed. It can be programmed to turn lights on and off if you are gone for extended periods of time. Smart light bulbs can also regulate themselves based on daylight availability. Exterior low-voltage lighting can be managed by app and will respond based on available light.

Music & Video – Inside & Outside

Smart home media technology connects to the internet and controls your music and video throughout the interior of your home and the exterior landscaping, patio and pool areas. Speakers and devices that play your favorite music and video on demand and can be voice and/or app controlled.

Locks - Doors & Garage Doors

With a smart lock and smart garage door opener you can grant access to visitors through your phone app. Smart locks can also detect if someone is near and unlock the doors for them.

Video/Audio Survelliance

Smart security cameras allow you to monitor your home when you are not there (and even when you are there). Smart motion sensors can turn on lights, engage the camera/audio function and even notify the police.

Heating & Air Conditioning

Smart thermostats can schedule, monitor and remotely control home temperatures and humidity. These devices can also learn your behaviors and automatically change settings for your comfort. Smart thermostats can remind you when to change filters and give you a report on your energy use. They can also be connected to your ceiling fans for turning them on and off. Smart heating and air conditioning apps are critical for an energy-saving home.

Kitchen Appliances

Smart coffee makers that brew you a fresh cup when your alarm goes off or at a pre-determined time. Refrigerators that make shopping lists, keep track of expiration dates, and even create recipes based on ingredients currently on hand! Even pet care can be automated with connected feeders to dispense food and water.

Landscaping

All landscaping can be controlled by smart in-ground irrigation systems.

Home Sensors

Power surges basically come from three sources: the electric company, lightening or when a large appliance like an air conditioner or refrigerator motor turns on and off. Power surges can enter a home through several paths. It doesn't always come in through the electrical service line. In the case of lightening, it can take the path of the cable TV or satellite dish cable, telephone lines or the electric service line. A good protection system should include: protection of the incoming electrical service, some type of protection of phone lines and cable TV lines and point-of-use surge protectors at sensitive and expensive appliances. Always engage a licensed electrician for this type of work.

Water disasters can be mitigated with smart sensor controls for water failure or freezing pipes that turn water off. These products run the gamut from just notifying you through an app that water or freezing is detected, to the more sophisticated systems that actually detect and then turn the water off in your home.

Security

Of course, security issues abound...hackers and privacy are the two main issues. Before implementing any new technology in your home, be sure to understand how to protect access to your home and the information in your home.

19 HOME MAINTENANCE CALENDAR

HOME SAFETY & MAINTENANCE	SPRING	FALL	ANNUAL	AS NEEDED	CALL A PRO
Check your smoke detectors	✔	✔			
Check carbon monoxide detectors	✔	✔			
Check your dryer vent for clogs	✔	✔			
Have your wood burning chimney inspected		✔		✔	✔
Check fire extinguishers			✔		
Have radon levels tested			✔		
Check that garage door openers work properly	✔	✔			
Look around property for tripping hazards (especially in a garage)	✔	✔			
Check emergency preparedness kit	✔				
If you have fuel cans stored, check them for safety	✔	✔			
Check water heater temperature			✔		
Have water tested			✔		✔

PLUMBING	SPRING	FALL	ANNUAL	AS NEEDED	CALL A PRO
Locate your water shut off valves & exercise them			✔		
Have your water conditioning equipment checked			✔		✔
Check your well system, if you have one	✔	✔			
Have your backflow preventers checked by a professional			✔		✔
Check your water meter for any leaks or sweating		✔			
Check your drains for speed of drainage (water should fully swirl)			✔		
Run water into any unused bathroom sinks or other sinks			✔		
Treat your drains with Bio-Clean®				Monthly	
Check sump pump and check valve for proper operation	✔	✔			
Check water heater for rust, wetness, etc.				Monthly	
Check water heater temperature (120 degrees at most)			✔		
Check traps and drains for sinks, tubs, showers for leaks			✔		
Check toilets for leaks with water color			✔		
Clean garbage disposal				Monthly	
Clean shower drain	✔	✔			
Clean showerhead	✔	✔			
Turn water off when leaving home for extended time				Vacations	

HEATING AND AIR CONDITIONING	SPRING	FALL	ANNUAL	AS NEEDED	CALL A PRO
Change your ceiling fan to appropriate setting	√	√			
Remove or cover window air conditioners		√			
Change your heating/AC filters	√	√		Monthly	
Dust around all air ducts				Monthly	
Check your dehumidifier for safe operation	√				
Check boiler for leaks		√			
Have your heating/AC systems tuned up	√	√			

ROOFS, GUTTERS, ATTICS, VENTS, DECKS, SIDING	SPRING	FALL	ANNUAL	AS NEEDED	CALL A PRO
Clean out gutters and downspouts	√	√			
Make sure all gutters discharge water away from home		√			
Visually inspect roof for missing/damaged shingles	√	√			
Check all flashing to make sure it is secure	√	√			
Check all for signs of water infiltration	√				
Check that fans still exhaust to outdoors (ductwork)		√			
Check attic for adequate ventilation and insulation	√	√			
Check for signs of leaks where deck attaches to house	√				
Check that the fireplace damper works correctly		√		√	
Check any fences on the property for problems	√				
Check exterior areas for fall or tripping hazards	√	√			
Check property for rodents, bats, termites, carpenter bees	√	√			
Clean out window wells of leaves and check drainage	√	√			

WINDOWS, SKYLIGHTS, FLOORS & DOORS	SPRING	FALL	ANNUAL	AS NEEDED	CALL A PRO
Inspect windows and skylights for leaks	✓	✓		✓	
Inspect windows & doors for proper operation, lubricate if needed			✓		
Look for loose hinges and doorknobs and make repairs				✓	
Inspect garage doors for proper operation and safety	✓	✓			
Repair broken or cracked glass in any window or door	✓			✓	

FOUNDATIONS & BASEMENTS	SPRING	FALL	ANNUAL	AS NEEDED	CALL A PRO
Inspect foundations and basement for leaks	✓	✓		✓	
Test the radon levels in the basement			✓		
Inspect any floor drains for proper operation	✓	✓			
Check for rodents, bats, roaches, termites	✓	✓			

PAINT & TILE	SPRING	FALL	ANNUAL	AS NEEDED	CALL A PRO
Check shower and tub surrounds for signs of damage			✓		
Check floor tiles for any sign of movement			✓		
Check all grout and caulk throughout home	✓	✓			
Check all walls, window sills for signs of mold	✓	✓			

ELECTRICAL	SPRING	FALL	ANNUAL	AS NEEDED	CALL A PRO
Test all GFCI and AFCI outlets				Monthly	
Check bath and kitchen fans for safe operation	√	√			
Check electrical cords for overheating, loose connections, corrosion			√	√	
Check your electrical panel for correct labels and safe operation			√	√	
Before holidays, check all holiday electrical decorations for safety.				Holidays	

GENERATORS	SPRING	FALL	ANNUAL	AS NEEDED	CALL A PRO
Check your portable generator for safety	√	√		√	
Make sure the fuel for the portable generator is stored safely				√	
Check your whole house generator for safety	√	√			√

CHIMNEY & EXHAUST PIPES	SPRING	FALL	ANNUAL	AS NEEDED	CALL A PRO
Check your dryer vents for clogs and kinks			√		
Have dryer vent cleaned			√		√
Inspect your pipe flanges on the roof for rotting			√		
If you have a wood burning fireplace, get it inspected		√			√

SEPTIC SYSTEMS	SPRING	FALL	ANNUAL	AS NEEDED	CALL A PRO
Inspect plumbing lines, tank, access holes, drainfield	✓	✓		✓	
Have entire system inspected by a professional				Every 2-3 years	✓
Have your septic tank pumped out				Every 2-3 years	✓

APPLIANCES	SPRING	FALL	ANNUAL	AS NEEDED	CALL A PRO
Check water hoses on clothes washer			✓		
Check water hoses on refrigerator icemaker			✓		
Check water hoses on dishwasher			✓		
Clean dishwasher on inside	✓			✓	
Clean oven				✓	
Clean kitchen exhaust hood and air filter	✓	✓			
Clean clothes washing machine				Monthly	
Clean dryer vent filter	✓				
Vacuum coils behind refrigerator	✓				

Notes

118

General Plumbing

- Shut off water main and other isolation valves for toilets, sinks, laundry areas.
- Unclog sink drain/trap.
- Adjust the toilet float to stop the toilet from running.
- Use the right plunger.
- Caulk and grout a tub / sink.
- Shut off valves to any gas appliances.

Electrical/Heating & AC

- Install/replace smoke/CO detectors; change batteries.
- Trip and re-set breakers.
- Re-set GFCI outlets.
- Change a light bulb. Convert to low voltage bulbs.
- Set/adjust programmable thermostat.
- Change HVAC filters.
- Tape leaky air duct.
- Light the pilot light.

Carpentry/Paint/Maintenance

- Hammer a nail to hang artwork – so it will not fall down and still be level.
- Change/tighten door knob hinges.
- Spackle, sand and paint.
- Disable an automatic garage door to work manually (and re-engage by adjusting the sensor on the door).
- Powerwash your house, deck or patio.

Miscellaneous

- Hook the TV and DVD cable up.
- Hook up video game system.
- Jump start a car.
- Shovel snow without hurting your back.
- Operate a gas grill and change the fuel tank.

21 28 TOOLS EVERY WOMAN SHOULD KNOW HOW TO USE

Fire Extinguisher
Safety goggles
5 in 1 tool
Duct tape
WD-40
Adjustable wrench
Channel lock pliers
10 in 1 screwdriver
Tape measure
Level
Needle nose pliers
Vise grips
Hammer (different sizes)
Prybar/Flatbar

Utility and/or razor knife
Cordless drill and bits
Spackle and putty knife
Paint brushes / rollers
Caulk
Light weight aluminum ladder
Flashlight
Ice scraper for car windshield
Garbage pail with wheels
Plunger
Tool Belt
5 gallon bucket
Stud Finder
Cork Screw

APPENDIX

FORMS EVERYONE
SHOULD HAVE

If you have a renovation project, make sure the contractor gives you as much detail as possible.

SAMPLE SCOPE OF WORK
FOR BATHROOM & CLOSET REMODEL

Bathroom & Hall Closet

DEMOLITION
* Provide dust and floor protection throughout project.
* Remove mirror, medicine cabinets, lights, and accessories.
* Remove tub, tub tile and substrate.
* Remove vanity, top, sink, and toilet.
* Remove floor tile.
* Remove flooring underlayment.
* Remove drywall from walls and ceiling.
* Dispose of related debris.

CARPENTRY
* Supply and install new recessed 80 CFM fan with LED light.
* Connect fan to existing vent hood with new ductwork.
* Open and close floor to allow for plumbing changes.
* Screw new and existing subfloor to joists.
* Frame new partition wall for shower.
* Open wall to hallway and frame for door.
* Frame water closet wall shut.
* Frame new linen closet as per plans.
* Supply and install new plywood underlayment.
* Install necessary fire blocking/safing.
* Supply and install new drywall on walls and ceiling of bathroom and closet.
* Tape, spackle, sand and prep walls and ceilings for paint.
* Supply and install new cement board on shower walls.
* Supply and install new shower system and membrane.
* Supply and install new uncoupling membrane to bathroom floor.
* Supply and install **owner selected** tiles with (2) corner shelves in standard square layout on shower walls.
* Supply and install **owner selected** tiles for decorative band on shower walls.
* Supply and install **owner selected** tiles in standard square layout on bathroom floor.
* Supply and install **owner selected** stone threshold.
* Grout and caulk all new tiles. Grout to have polymer additive.
* Supply and install white melamine shelving in bathroom and hall linen closets as per plans.
* Supply and install new stain grade flush doors similar to existing for hall/ linen closets.
* Supply and install new clear pine door casings.
* Supply and install new clear pine window casing and stool.
* Supply and install new clear base molding.
* Supply and install **owner selected** vanity.
* Supply and install **owner selected** quartz vanity tops & splashes.
* Supply and install **owner selected** accessories.
* Supply and install **owner selected** mirrors.
* Supply and install **owner selected** shower door.

PLUMBING

* Supply and rough in new supply and PVC DWV lines to accommodate double basin vanity, toilet, and shower.
* Relocate toilet, shower, and vanity as per plans.
* Supply and install **owner selected** one piece shower valve with diverter and trim.
* Supply and install **owner selected** hand held.
* Supply and install **owner selected** slide bar.
* Supply and install (2) **owner selected** faucet(s).
* Supply and install (2) **owner selected** sinks.
* Supply and install **owner selected** toilet.
* Supply and install new ¼ turn chrome stops at all fixtures.
* Supply and install new base heat cover for existing heat unit.
* Plumbing includes all miscellaneous standard pipes and fittings required to hook up fixtures.
* Provide temperature adjustment for final inspection.
* Test and inspect as required.

ELECTRIC

* Remove existing fixtures and switches.
* Install (4) new switches.
* Connect new fan light.
* Add switch for new fan / light.
* Supply and install (1) 6" recessed light.
* Supply / relocate (2) outlets for vanity
* Supply and install (2) **owner selected** light fixtures above vanities.
* Supply and install (1) LED surface mount light in hall closet.
* Replace all existing switches and outlets with owner selected color units.

PAINT

* Prime all new drywall and repairs.
* Supply and apply (2) coats of premium white paint to the bathroom ceiling, closet ceiling, and closet walls.
* Supply and apply (2) coats of (specified) paint to the bathroom walls.
* Stain and apply (2) coats of poly to the new casing, base molding and doors.

ESTIMATED COST: $

ALLOWANCES INCLUDED IN ESTIMATED COST ('owner selected'):

Plumbing fixtures	$
Vanity top	$
Shower door and installation	$
Tile	$
Vanity	$
Mirror / Med cabinets	$
Accessories	$
Light Fixtures	$
TOTAL	$

SAMPLE SCOPE OF WORK FOR KITCHEN

Kitchen Renovation

DEMOLITION
- ✦ Provide dust and floor protection throughout project.
- ✦ Remove and dispose of kitchen cabinets, tops, soffit, vinyl flooring, crown and base moldings, brick wall and back splash, range hood, closet door, shelving and necessary drywall.
- ✦ Temporarily relocate appliances.

CARPENTRY
- ✦ Secure all existing subflooring to framing with screws.
- ✦ Supply and install 1/2" underlayment.
- ✦ Supply and install blocking as necessary.
- ✦ Supply and install drywall on walls and ceiling where removed.
- ✦ Tape, spackle, sand and prep for paint.
- ✦ Supply and install uncoupling membrane.
- ✦ Supply and install **owner selected** tile flooring.
- ✦ Grout new floor tiles. Grout to be mixed with grout shield.
- ✦ Supply and install new similar base molding.
- ✦ Supply and install **owner selected** cabinets as per plan.
- ✦ Supply and install **owner selected** hardware.
- ✦ Supply and install **owner selected** countertops.
- ✦ Supply and install **owner selected** tile backsplash.
- ✦ Grout new backsplash tiles. Grout to have polymer additive.
- ✦ Install *owner supplied* venting microwave.
- ✦ Extend microwave vent line through roof and install new vent hood.
- ✦ Supply and install floating shelves in old closet location.

PLUMBING
- ✦ Supply and install new supply lines for kitchen sink and ice maker.
- ✦ Relocate and install new gas lines for range.
- ✦ Supply and install new ¼ turn chrome shut off valves for sink and dishwasher.
- ✦ Supply and install ice maker line.
- ✦ Connect ice maker line to refrigerator.
- ✦ Drain, shorten and fill heat loop to allow for additional cabinets.
- ✦ Supply and install **owner selected** undermount kitchen sink.
- ✦ Supply and install **owner selected** faucet.
- ✦ Install *owner supplied* dishwasher.
- ✦ Install *owner supplied* gas range.
- ✦ Reconnect original washing machine and dryer.
- ✦ Plumbing includes standard pipe and fittings to make all connections.

ELECTRIC

✦ Supply and install (4) 6" LED recessed lights.
✦ Supply and install (2) ceiling boxes.
✦ Supply and install (8) new outlets for counter, peninsula, refrigerator, dishwasher, range, and microwave.
✦ Supply and install (2) new dimmer switches.
✦ Supply and install outlet and cord for dishwasher.
✦ Supply and install dedicated microwave outlet and breaker.
✦ Install (3) **owner selected** light fixtures.
✦ Install new _owner supplied_ ceiling fan.

PAINT

✦ Prime all new drywall and repairs.
✦ Apply (2) coats of (specified) paint to the kitchen ceiling.
✦ Apply (2) coats of (specified) paint to the kitchen walls.
✦ Stain and apply (2) coats of polyurethane to new base molding

ESTIMATED COST: $_____ +
Permits

Price subject to material selections and final layout.

ALLOWANCES INCORPORATED INTO ESTIMATE COST ('owner selected'):

Cabinets	$
Hardware	$
Countertops	$
Tile	$
Lights	$
Shelving	$
Sink	$
Faucet	$

Total Allowances $_____

FULL WAIVER AND RELEASE OF LIEN

"STATE OF _____)
COUNTY OF _____) "

Project Name:_____
Invoice #:_____

TO WHOM IT MAY CONCERN:

The undersigned subcontractor (_____) has been employed by
_____(contractor name) who in turn is employed by:
_____ (homeowner name) to furnish labor and
material at the premises located at _____(work address).

The undersigned, for and in consideration of sums received in the amount of $_____and other good and
valuable consideration, which together represent the value of work completed and installed, hereby waives and releases
any and all liens, or claims or rights to liens, under the laws of the State of New Jersey relating to mechanic's liens, with
respect to and on the above-described premises and the improvements thereon, and on the material fixtures, apparatus or
machinery finished, and on the moneys, funds or other considerations due or to become due from the Owner and/or
Leasehold Tenant or account of labor, services, material fixtures, apparatus or machinery, furnished by the undersigned for
the above-described project.

The undersigned further represents and warrants that s/he is duly authorized and empowered to sign and execute
this waiver and release on his/her own behalf and on behalf of the company or business for which s/he is signing; that it has
properly performed all work and furnished all the materials of the specified quality in accordance with the contract
documents in a good and workmanlike manner, fully and completely; that it has paid for all labor, materials equipment and
services that it has used or supplied or may hereafter use or supply to the above-described premises; that it has no other
outstanding and unpaid payment applications, invoices, retentions, holdbacks, expenses employed in the prosecution of
work, charge backs or unbilled work or materials against the Owner and/or the Leasehold Tenant; and that any materials
which have been supplied or incorporated into the above premises were either taken from its fully-paid or open stock or
were fully paid for and supplied as stated on the partial invoice.

The undersigned further agrees to defend, indemnify and hold harmless the Owner and/or the Leasehold Tenant
for any losses or expenses, should any such claim, lien or right to a lien be asserted by any of the undersigned's laborers,
materialmen or subcontractors.

The undersigned further waives, releases and relinquishes any and all claims, rights or causes of action in equity
or law whatsoever arising out of, through or under the above-mentioned project and the performance of work pursuant
thereto.

IN WITNESS WHEREOF, the undersigned subcontractor has caused this instrument to be signed by its officer
thereunto duly authorized this date: _____

*Work performed: please give summary or reference description of work

_____

Sworn to before me this _____ day
of _____, 2016

By: _____ **(sign)**

_____
Print Name

_____
Notary Public, State of

_____
Print Company

CONTRACTOR EVALUATION FORM
Contractor Name, Address, Phone Contact Information

_____
_____
_____
_____
_____
_____
_____
_____
_____
_____

Contractor License Numbers

_____

Contractor Insurance Information

(Liability, Auto & Workman's Compensation)

_____
_____
_____
_____

Questions to ask the prospective contractor.

1. Who owns the business & how long have you been in business?

2. Are you involved in the local Chamber of Commerce, other local business groups or a national trade association?

3. Are you licensed in your state, as required? What licenses? Get copies of licenses.

4. How many projects like mine have you completed in the last year?

5. May I have a list of references from those projects?

6. Can I visit a prior customer's job to see a finished product?

7. May I have a list of business referrals and suppliers?

8. What percentage of your business is repeat or referral business?

9. Does your company carry worker's compensation and liability insurance? Do all of your sub contractors have the appropriate insurance? Get copies of certificates of insurance from the general contractor and the sub contractors.

10. Will building permits be required for my project? Most projects require inspections for building, plumbing, fire, electric, and some projects need to be submitted to your local Zoning and Health Department for approval as well. Before you even ask the contractor this question, you can visit your local Building Department and ask them. Then you can verify what the contractor tells you.

11. Who will be assigned as project supervisor for the job?

12. Who will be working on the project? Get names of employees and subcontractors.

13. What is your approach to a project such as this?

14. How long will it take for my project from start to finish?

15. What kind of "unexpected" expenses are expected?

16. How do you handle the "dirty work" of dust containment?

17. Will you be providing a written contract with the following?
    a. details of the job (including product specifications)
    b. a breakdown of costs by labor and materials
    c. list of sub contractors and their insurance
    d. how change orders are handled
    e. payment schedule & right to cancel clause
    f. written warranties
    g. project start and end date

Here are some other things to think about as you are evaluating a company.

1. Did they show up on time?

2. Were they wearing company apparel?

3. Does their truck have the business name, phone number and license numbers required?

4. Did they offer a business card and/or other company marketing material?

5. Did they bring a camera or tablet to take photos?

6. Did they take measurements?

7. Did they tell you a range of costs for your project?

8. Did they give you a timeframe for the completion of the estimate?

EQUIPMENT FORM

Furnace
    Make   _____
    Model   _____
    Serial #   _____
    Year Installed_____
    Type   Gas_____   Electric_____   Heat Pump_____
    Size   _____

Air Conditioner
    Make   _____
    Model   _____
    Serial #   _____
    Year Installed_____
    Type   Gas_____   Electric_____   Heat Pump_____
    Size   _____

Water Heater
    Make   _____
    Model   _____
    Serial #   _____
    Year Installed_____
    Type   Gas_____   Electric_____   Heat Pump_____
    Size   _____

Water Conditioning
    Make   _____
    Model   _____
    Serial #   _____
    Year Installed_____
    Size   _____

Sump Pump
    Make   _____
    Model   _____
    Serial #   _____
    Year Installed_____
    Size   _____

Humidifier
    Make   _____
    Model   _____
    Serial #   _____
    Year Installed_____

Generator
    Make   _____
    Model   _____
    Serial #   _____
    Year Installed_____
    Type   Natural Gas_____ Propane_____
    Size   _____

Washing Machine
    Make   _____
    Model   _____
    Serial #   _____
    Year Installed_____

Dryer
    Make   _____
    Model   _____
    Serial #   _____
    Year Installed_____

Refrigerator
    Make   _____
    Model   _____
    Serial #   _____
    Year Installed_____

Stove/Oven
    Make   _____
    Model   _____
    Serial #   _____
    Year Installed_____

Made in the USA
Middletown, DE
18 September 2019